WHITE BOOTS
& MINISKIRTS

A TRUE STORY OF LIFE IN THE SWINGING SIXTIES FROM
THE AUTHOR OF BESTSELLING *BOMBSITES & LOLLIPOPS*

JACKY HYAMS

JOHN BLAKE

Published by John Blake Publishing Ltd,
3 Bramber Court, 2 Bramber Road,
London W14 9PB, England

www.johnblakepublishing.co.uk

www.facebook.com/Johnblakepub facebook
twitter.com/johnblakepub twitter

First published in paperback in 2013

ISBN: 9781782190141

British Library Cataloguing-in-Publication Data:

A catalogue record for this book is available from the British Library.

Design by www.envydesign.co.uk

Printed and bound in Great Britain by CPI Group (UK) Ltd

1 3 5 7 9 10 8 6 4 2

© Text copyright Jacky Hyams, 2013

Papers used by John Blake Publishing are natural, recyclable
products made from wood grown in sustainable forests.
The manufacturing processes conform to the environmental
regulations of the country of origin.

To Ron, Clive and Ian.
Gone too soon. But not forgotten.

CONTENTS

FOREWORD

My sincere thanks to the usual suspects, fellow writers Tammy Cohen, for her unfailing support and insight, and John Parrish in Sydney, whose enthusiasm for my ideas never fails to encourage me.

All thanks also go to Alice Jordan (for showing me that the life of a 20-something woman hasn't changed that much!) and to Mary Bowen, my Melbourne *consigliere*, always up for consultation – and excellent advice.

Gratitude too to Jenny Wright and Jeff Samuels, former news desk inmates whose memories of those times proved invaluable.

Finally, a big thank you to the British Library team at Colindale, unfailingly courteous and polite, no matter how minor the request.

INTRODUCTION

The country was going to the dogs. Optimism was in short supply. The economy was in a perilous place. Money was tight. Upheaval on the streets. House price crash. Terrorism. And unemployment on the rise...

Welcome to Britain. Go on, fill in the year. Some time in the early 21st century, perhaps? Yes and no. Because our history is dotted with similar patches of extreme uncertainty when the only way through seems to be to either just get on with it – somehow – or get out, jump on a plane, find a better way of life... Back in 1976, when I decided to do just that, the country was pretty much locked into a negative spiral: the general belief was that Britain had a dismal future.

Yet just ten years before, the sun shone down on Blighty and the streets were full of partying people: the summer's World Cup soccer victory over Germany at

Wembley in 1966 seemed to set the seal on what looked like a golden age of optimism. Mini-skirted London was widely acknowledged as the swinging city. An unprecedented explosion of Brit creativity had made a huge impact all over the world. Our musicians, designers, pop and movie stars were fast becoming international icons. Youth culture was big news, on the march, especially across the Atlantic.

The older, wartime generation might have blinked, rubbed their eyes at all these long hair and free love ideas that were being spouted, let alone the idea of their kids hitting the hippie trail to the East or smoking pot, but these were stable times: jobs for nearly everyone, less than a quarter of a million people unemployed in that year of World Cup jubilation. Foreign holidays in the sun had started to become a national pastime. And colour telly was on its way.

When I sat down in 2011 to write my 1950s East End memoir of my childhood, *Bombsites and Lollipops*, I wrote not just about myself, my parents, my teenage adventures, but about the world I'd inhabited, one of a society – and a city – shaking off the lingering effect and deprivations of wartime and very slowly reinventing itself into something approaching what we know today. I had hoped, of course, that readers could identify with some of it or that if the world described was unfamiliar, even alien, they'd find something entertaining in the reminiscence of the 'lost world'.

Much to my delight, they did. The response was immensely gratifying. A writer always hopes to strike the right chord, but you never really know if you've hit the right note until you get the feedback from your readers. Among all the welcome positive feedback, I kept getting the same comments, time and time again: 'So what happened next?', 'How did you get from there to here?', 'I didn't want it to end'. And so on. Hence my decision to write a sequel, covering another lost world, the decade after that book ended, when I'd first left home and started to make my way in life.

The changes in my own life were gradual. But in some ways, they were reflections of the big social changes around me. And the mood of the country itself shifted quite quickly: from chirpy to bleak within a few years. In the summer of 1966, anything seemed possible, the future looked good. Yet even by 1970, the storm clouds were already gathering. Everyday lives were changing for the good, more people travelled abroad, wages were good and though it was early days, the arrival of the supermarket and the home ownership culture were already making an impact. Yet from then on, industrial disputes, strikes, shortages and inflationary woes were to continuously plunge the country into crisis mode through the decade.

The '60s – the sex, drugs and rock'n'roll years – are always viewed as the pivotal moment, the starting gun, if you like, of massive change in British society. Technically, this was true. Yet a lot of it was mostly hype: the much-touted sexual revolution, at least, didn't actually happen for most people until the '70s arrived. And the politics of the time, from Harold Wilson's rocky Labour era of 1964-70 to the false dawn of the Conservative 'Better times ahead' Ted Heath years that followed, eventually took the country down a bitterly acrimonious path of union confrontation and IRA terrorist carnage. If the '60s seemed like the best of times, the decade that followed surely would seem the worst of times.

That extraordinary decade followed the years of my youth. The immediate post- WWII generation were late starters by today's standards. We lost our virginity in our late teens, maybe later. We emerged from the late '50s as the first wave of youthful consumers, even though, as teenagers, we hardly knew what consumerism signified. For those like me, abandoning education at 16, it could be said that our university years were the march straight into the adult working world. Through work, you meet people. Move around all the time from job to job, as I did, and you meet many more, learning as you go, not just about offices but about life. Constant exposure to lots of different people from many different backgrounds hadn't always been the common experience for working class girls – until the class barriers started to wobble in the '60s.

I was a rebel, in that I wanted to throw off my East End background and didn't accept the general status quo: that a young girl best sit tight and hang on for Mr Right. Yet I wasn't in any way political in my thinking. My ideas about freedom and free love weren't feminist as such. I didn't go on marches or protest on the streets. I didn't consciously believe women's lot was unfair. Certainly, I questioned what I'd been told since childhood, mainly because a lot of it didn't make sense to me. Fortunately, I was single-minded in my determination to reject all this by getting out there, sharing flats, though without real economic independence, the very thing I craved, this didn't always prove to be a successful venture. How could it be? I wasn't an educated thinker. I operated on instinct alone, an ordinary 20-something from a challenging background at a time when women were just starting to be unshackled from the many things that had always held them back: fear of unwanted pregnancy, outdated laws around divorce, economic restraint. For me, it was all about having my freedom.

Around the time my story starts, a single mum was in a bad place as far as the rest of the world was concerned. Some men still believed they had to tell a woman they loved her in order to convince her it was OK to have sex. Yet by 1976, 'I love you' was frequently being replaced by 'What was your name again?' the morning after. Or 'I divorce you'. By then, anyone landing from a distant planet could have easily wondered if many of the inhabitants of these islands had anything else on their mind other than sex. Or hedonism.

Working lives changed a lot too in that decade. In 1966, most men preferred to have stay-at-home wives. Ten years on, a woman's work or part-time job to supplement the household income, help pay the bills to raise their family, was more or less taken for granted. My belief too is that in this transitional decade, younger people, at least, became much more worldly in outlook. The cheap travel had a lot to do with that. The '70s kick started the real changes in what we ate back home too, reflected by the many Chinese, Italian, Indian and Greek restaurants that started to pop up on our streets. Whether we liked it or not (and many did not) the switch to a decimal currency followed by Britain's entry into the European Economic Community (EEC) in 1973 shifted our general perspective a notch, forced us to look outwards.

This is, of course, a personal story. It's about my own experiences and what was going on around me. London is a huge, sprawling city: very much a series of villages and my personal village had distinct borders. It encompassed my parents' home in Dalston, central London, the West End, Fleet Street and the leafier parts of north-west London. It certainly wasn't suburbia. But what is interesting about it in historical terms, if you like, is that many of those streets and places where the story took place remain just as they were.

Fleet Street, of course, has vanished in that it's no longer a thoroughfare hosting most of the country's national newspapers, but an extension of the financial and legal district, though a few of the ancient pubs still remain as testament to journalism's long lamented pub culture. The huge *Mirror* building where I worked, the proud, bustling enterprise which dominated the area around Holborn and Chancery Lane for so many years, is gone, the site transformed into Sainsbury's head office. Which probably speaks volumes about the changes to our way of life. And there are the areas around Hackney and Dalston: left virtually untouched for several decades, they're now dramatically changed by a wave of gentrification, infrastructure and fashionable development, something that was unimaginable in the shabby, scruffy '70s.

The music was there all the time, too. Originally an Elvis girl, I remained loyal. For life. Yet what followed Elvis musically became such a phenomenon – I defy anyone around in 1967 not to remember where they were or what they were doing the first time they heard the *Sgt Pepper's…* album. The music resonates still. The wonderful thing about it is we can now access it instantly, with a touch of a button or a single swipe. If anything, the music takes on an even greater significance the more time passes. It was that good: listen to it now and marvel at the extraordinary talent that produced it. Yet at the time, for me, it was just… taken for granted. Like all the other exciting things that were happening around us.

There are places in my memory where the detail is somewhat cloudy (this book does start in the '60s, after all). So I trust I'll be forgiven for that. Some names have been changed too. My single regret in this is that I didn't write it all down at the time. But here, at least, are some of the highs and lows of those times remembered. We laughed a lot, drank and smoked too much, slept too little and lived, mostly, for the next party. Or holiday in the sun. It might have been almost half a century ago. Yet the carefree, often reckless insouciance of youth never changes. Mine was definitely prolonged by my refusal to take responsibility for anything. Yet for that, I am now truly grateful. There was time enough ahead to sober up and start living sensibly.

I like to regard that 1960s–70s decade as the era when many of us happily followed the hedonistic 'Have a good time – all of the time' mantra (as put so eloquently in the rock'n'roll movie *This is Spinal Tap*).

Though of course you can, if you wish, use those words as a motto for life…

Jacky Hyams
London, February 2013

THE STORY SO FAR

In my previous book *Bombsites and Lollipops*, I told the story of my childhood, growing up in post-WW2 Hackney in one of London's most deprived, bomb scarred areas in the East End. With my parents, Molly and Ginger, I inhabited a bizarre world. We lived in squalid, depressing surroundings: a tiny, damp flat in a narrow alleyway dotted with bombsites and ruined buildings. Poverty was all around us in the 1950s, yet we lived like kings. While most of the country skimped and saved, struggling to live on meagre rations, enduring freezing winters, fuel shortages and power cuts, we ate the very best food available, wore beautiful clothes, had an army of servants and helpers – including a cleaner and a chauffeur – and my parents stepped out frequently, living the high life in London's West End or partying with London's most notorious duo: the Kray Twins.

Our lavish lifestyle was courtesy of my grandfather Jack's booming Petticoat Lane business as a bookmaker. Returning from WW2, my dad Ginger joined his father in what was then a thriving illegal trade, taking bets in the East End's pubs and streets from the hordes of punters and street traders whose daily gambling on the 'gee-gees' and dogs was part of a way of life. Ginger's pockets were constantly stuffed with wads of cash, mostly blown on a wild, post-War spending spree that never seemed to end.

As for me, I grew up a spoilt, only child, indulged by

my hedonistic parents in a bewildering world where money was no object, yet at the same time surrounded by a grim, grey backdrop. The city was gradually struggling to its feet. Initially a studious child, once at grammar school I morphed into a rebellious, stroppy teen in the Elvis era.

By the dawn of the '60s, I'd abandoned my studies and was working in offices in London's West End, hanging out in Soho after hours and moving from job to job as I started to travel, learn about life and seek love and adventure in the wider world beyond Hackney. The inevitable teenage clashes with my dad, whose heavy drinking, possessive ways and free spending habits led him down a perilous path, saw me desperate to get away from home and break free of my claustrophobic environment.

Yet it wasn't until 1966 that I finally got away and found freedom of sorts in a shared flat in north-west London. My dad's bookie world collapsed around him and London itself was beginning to be transformed into the world's most 'swinging' city.

CHAPTER ONE
THE COMPLAINTS MANAGER

A light aircraft, a Piper Aztec, is taking off from a small airfield just outside London.

It's a clear, bright summer weekend afternoon, a light breeze, little cloud, remarkably good flying conditions. As the plane climbs to 2,000 feet, anyone looking up from below might envy the passengers the delight of their winged freedom on this, a perfect day. If they continued to look up, they might have been somewhat impressed by the daring but perfectly executed aerobatic roll executed by the pilot a few minutes later.

Brilliant stuff. If you're on the ground. But I'm up in the tiny plane, strapped in behind the pilot, Des, and his friend, Jeff. A gregarious, charismatic, speedy chatter-upper in his early thirties, Jeff is hell bent on making a real impression on me, a 21-year-old secretary working in his office. Well, it's one way to pull the birds, eh? Persuade your best mate, a former RAF fighter pilot, to take you and your latest object of desire up in the clouds for a few aerobatic show-off manoeuvres.

'Show Jacky some tricks, Jeffrey,' laughs Des, as he manoeuvres the controls to send us into that head spinning, stomach-churning, 360-degree spin. Luckily, I'm not expecting this. No time to anticipate the sheer terror of being flipped upside down in a flimsy airborne tin can: it's all over in a matter of seconds. I manage to remain impassive, stay outwardly remote, in my gingham mini-dress with the white organdie collar, cutaway shoulders and short white Courrèges boots, though it's the fake cool of ignorant youth, rather than any kind of real courage or bravado, that gets me through this terrifying moment. This is the sort of thing that's exciting once you've done it, I tell myself. He could've asked me first…

'All right Miss Hyams?' grins Jeff, turning back to give my exposed bare knee a quick caress. Jeff's a Hackney lad, common ground with me that he's exploiting to the hilt in his quest, so far thwarted, to get me into bed.

'Yeah,' I smile, remembering to show my girly gratitude to my host. 'Er… nice one, Des.'

'Next time we'll show her some more tricks, eh Jeff?' winks Des as he expertly handles the controls and guides the plane down towards the landing strip. Jeff looks chuffed: 'tricks' are his thing all right. I'm well used to the double entendre: it goes on all day, every day in the office. But I'm not the giggly, wriggly, 'Oo, you are awful' type. It's usually a sarcastic retort, a sharp put down. Yet today, for some reason, I don't bite back.

Still, for 1966, this is a pretty resourceful ploy for seduction. Getting young women up in small planes isn't exactly commonplace. Nor is flying itself, still mostly for the comfortably off, though I've already had my first flight to Italy and, by the end of the decade, five million Brits will be off holidaying abroad, mainly on package-deal charter flights.

Mostly, men deploy their cars as girl bait, especially those who can afford to show off in flash Rovers, souped-up Minis, Triumph TR4s or MG MGBs. Young office girls are still some way off from buying their own cars after they pass the test, propelling themselves around town independently. And because it is still quite common for sons and daughters to live in the family home until marriage, car ownership means a guy has, at least, a love trap on wheels. Otherwise it's outdoor sex (never a brilliant idea in Blighty's climate, but nonetheless popular because it's comparatively easy to find a secluded spot to carefully place the blanket) or the deserted office or shop floor – more popular then than you'd ever imagine. Or, as a final resort, there's always the family home when unoccupied: not always achievable with other siblings hanging around.

Jeff hasn't yet quite convinced me of his charms on

this day of the aerobatic somersault. He's an outrageous flirt around the electronics company where we both work and there's an element of mystery around his existence that makes me initially wary (it will take several years before I learn to trust those first, crucial instincts).

He claims to live with a brother, somewhere in deepest Hertfordshire. The truth is he lives in sin in Pinner with a much older woman he's been with for years. There's also an illegitimate son and the boy's mother, tucked away in Scotland, seen about once a year – a brief affair from Jeff's national service days. Yet I don't know about any of this when, a few months later, I willingly succumb to his persistent advances in the back of his Rover.

This relationship with Jeff, which continues until I learn the whole truth a couple of years later, brings my tally of boyfriends up to three. There's Bryan, the on–off boyfriend, a racy, chubby advertising man I knew before leaving home in Dalston. I go to pubs, Indian or Chinese restaurants with Bryan and sleep with him, usually in his flat, albeit intermittently. And recently, I've regularly started to see Martin, a less dashing figure than the other two – a wiry, ambitious shop manager from Islington, a sharp dresser, almost a Mod, whom I mostly see on weekends for drives and trips to the cinema.

It sounds odd now, but our favourite drive is to get into Martin's much-prized Mini and drive to Heathrow airport (people actually drove to airports then just to look at the planes, a popular family day out). Today's traffic-clogged, hellish and unloved route from central London to Heathrow, the A4, was very different then, virtually empty and car-free. Sometimes we whizz down from central London to the airport in 20 minutes or so. No unending stream of planes taking off every 60 seconds at Heathrow then. Park outside, go into the quiet terminal, blissfully free of innumerable shopping opportunities and sit there, watching the BEA Comets and the Spantax Coronados. Without the crowds and bustle we know today, it is all quite… romantic. 'I'm gonna be on one of those BOAC planes one day, when I go to live in the States,' Martin says confidently. And he does just that a few years later.

I never do get too involved with Martin for some reason, though I admire his sparky determination to move his life along and not just accept what he's been dished out. Our dates never go beyond the odd snogging session in the Mini. Who knows? Maybe he had another girl, maybe he hid his shyness or lack of sexual experience under his sharp-suited exterior.

Yet had anyone asked me back then, I'd have told them it was perfectly acceptable for a young single woman to go out with – and sleep with – as many men as she pleased, get drunk if she felt like it and treat life like an adventure, a quest for experience, rather than a single-minded march towards marriage and motherhood. After all, it was 1966, wasn't it? Sex was now freely available. Thanks to the arrival of the contraceptive pill, women of all ages, single or married, no longer had to worry about the threat of unwanted pregnancy or men who couldn't abide johnnies. ('Like picking your nose with a boxing glove,' as one wag described it.)

The '60s, of course, are historically defined by the sexual revolution because once the pill was introduced (1961) and the laws on abortion changed (1967), sex became quite a different proposition, as women had real choice in such matters for the first time ever. All this sex revolution stuff was sweet music to my ears. Yet it was still a matter of time before those changes actually took effect in everyday lives: the reality across the land was not quite the way I was choosing to see it. Women's take up of the pill in the '60s was tiny: only one in ten were actually taking it by the end of the decade. If my conversations with girlfriends were anything to go by at that point, I was a little bit different to those I knew in being quite so generous with my favours. Some of us were bravely, blindly, diving into the freedom of choice or 'love is free if you want it' idea. But not half as many were going for it as one might imagine from the burble and hype around the sexual revolution and swinging London in the mid-1960s.

Today no one bats an eyelid at single women juggling lovers of either sex, having one night stands at whim or even opting for what are known, somewhat bleakly, as 'fuck buddies'. This kind of thing was not really happening for the majority in the mid-1960s. Essentially, the sexual freedom hype, as purveyed by the newspapers of the time (let's face it, it's an eye-catching story, particularly when there are pictures of beautiful young women in tiny skirts to go with it), created a somewhat confusing picture of a wild, free-love society which, to a greater extent, was still the very opposite: it remained solidly class-bound and reticent in all matters sexual. Youth was going mad, but for now the older generation was having none of it.

Nonetheless, the genie is well and truly out of the bottle. The influence of the maverick young leading the way, the Pied Pipers of the '60s, is enormous: the Beatles, Stones, snappers David Bailey and Terence Donovan, models Jean Shrimpton, Celia Hammond and Twiggy, actors such as Michael Caine and Terry Stamp, and girls like Cathy McGowan, the *Ready Steady Go* presenter with her glossy long hair and dead straight fringe. Mostly (but not quite all) they are working class, yet they are positioned right at the heart of all the hype by dint of what they represent – youth, glamour, talent and beautiful role models for millions of youngsters.

Beyond the buzzy, happening centre of London – just a few square miles of tiny clubs, shops, an area running from posh, louche Chelsea, the King's Road, the fabled, tiny Abingdon Road shop called Biba (which moves to Kensington High Street in 1965) and across to the West End and Soho – the swinging city runs out of steam. Out in the groovy live music venues in south-west

London's suburbs – the Bull's Head at Barnes (jazz) or the Crawdaddy in the Station Hotel, Richmond (the bluesy launch pad for the Rolling Stones) – there had been a buzz going since the early '60s. Yet way beyond, in the outer suburbs, the provincial cities or small towns, free love, long hair for men and dolly birds in micro minis are on their way – but have not yet arrived. Only by the time of the summer of love, 1967, the pivotal moment when the Beatles launched the groundbreaking *Sgt Pepper's Lonely Hearts Club Band* and young people started piling in to cool, small, trendy venues in cities and towns like Canterbury, Bristol, Norwich, York and, of course, Liverpool, was the effect of it all to move right across the country, fuelled by the massive influence of the music and those making it – and of the powerful American hippie culture.

Yet at this point, real economic freedom, as we know it now, is still a long way away for ordinary, working class girls like me. Career options for professional women remain limited, even for the university-educated middle classes. Beyond shop, factory or office and secretarial work there is – what? Nursing, teaching and the civil service, of course. And for the educated women, academia. A few middle-class women venture into creative fields like advertising or journalism, yet the limitations don't lift in the '60s. Girls' jobs remain more or less what you do before finding a man to marry, rather than the sometimes overblown career expectations of millions of young girls now, spurred on by fantastic dreams of instant stardom and lifelong riches.

I may be more rebellious in my thinking than the other girls I know of my age, some of whom are already married. In my case, however, I am a child of my times in that I am heavily influenced by the imagery and the printed word. Like so many others, I soak it all up. Because I have avoided further education and dived into the working world at 16, most of my ideas about life and sex come through devouring magazines like three-month-old US *Cosmopolitans*, eagerly purchased from Soho newsagents each month. (Britain's *Cosmo* does not arrive until 1972.)

US *Cosmo*, with its bold editor, Helen Gurley Brown (best quote: 'Bad girls go everywhere'), pushes forward the daring new belief that women can enjoy sex, pick and choose their partners – they don't have to focus solely on marriage and motherhood to lead a fulfilled life. They can make themselves gorgeous – and follow their own career path. This, to me, makes perfect sense. All of it. I already understand, by pure instinct, that the traditional path up the aisle isn't going to suit me. Too restrictive, too mundane. Men? Yes, please. Sex? Ooh, yes. Marriage? Er… no thanks. Babies? Pass. Though it will be many years before the notion of career ambition starts to emerge for me.

Yet for all my defiance and media-led ideas about sexual freedom, I am still stuck with one thing: the men around me continue to retain all the power. Even at this mid-1960s point when the social change really begins to accelerate, the men are still setting the agenda of the chase. You can reject an offer, an advance, a date. But if you like someone, fancy them, you still have to sit around waiting for the phone to ring, summoning you. It's a convention I profoundly resent, partly because I am terminally impatient but also because I see all this waiting as grossly unfair. My argument is: if you can phone me when you want, why can't I phone you? Yet because such equality doesn't yet exist and communication itself is so limited by today's standards – phone, letter or a knock on the door – I'm still stuck with that wait, staring at the black Bakelite instrument, willing it to send out its shrill, exciting sound.

This limited communication also gives men the edge in terms of keeping you in the dark about what they are actually up to. It's so much easier for them to be vague or non-committal. Or simply untruthful, which some '60s men are if they're juggling two 'birds' at a time. Unless they live or work near you, know your friends and family, how can you, living in the heart of the big city, know anything about what they're really doing? No Facebook, Google or website to check someone out. No blog, no exchange of text messages or tweets, mobile phone lists. No email to whizz off a swift one-line retort or naughty come-on. Telegrams, delivered to your front door, usually by bike, are the only other means of fast communication.

You can hardly send a telegram to a man: 'HURRY UP AND RING ME, YOU BASTARD'. Or even: 'WHAT'S GOING ON, IT'S BEEN TWO WEEKS SINCE YOU CALLED'.

Voicing these things out loud when the call does come never seems to get you anywhere. Just more waffle, excuses and vague references to 'work'. If a man you're entangled with says they're going 'up north on business' (a popular favourite in London, the frozen north being a remote place to be approached with considerable caution) for an unspecified period, you accept it. People simply could not go round checking up on each other's behaviour the way they do now. So '60s men, for all the historical hype about the era, got away with a lot that would be very difficult for them to get away with now. Unless you're going steady or engaged, the unspoken rule is: they call, you can't ring them.

Financially, too, they call the shots. Going Dutch or sharing the bill does not exist in traditional dating. The man pays for the drinks, the cinema seat, the meal, you drive there in his car – whatever needs to be paid for in cold cash is down to him. He's doing the courting (unless he's seriously mean, when it's just a drive and maybe one or two drinks, if you're lucky, in a local pub). The tradition of the man paying is reinforced by the fact that women earn much less than men and will continue to do so for a long time. Even in the rarer instances where there is some kind of equality of pay at work, you're unlikely to find anything other than misogyny from the men in charge. 'Equal pay, equal work, carry your own fucking typewriter' was the mantra of one friend's boss, an editor of a local newspaper when she joined the team as a youthful reporter.

You can, of course, invite a man round for a meal if you're not living at home – the idea of the 'dinner party' is already starting to take hold now that growing affluence and full employment are virtually taken for granted – but for me this is hardly a thank-you or even an invitation to seduction. It's more a way of expanding social horizons.

By now, I'm sharing a big flat in north-west London with three other girls where the rules of engagement with men are perpetuated. Our landlord had sensibly installed a coin-operated payphone inside the flat. After work it's permanently engaged (without even any 'call waiting' to get someone off the line). All a smitten girl has for comfort is the unimpeachable, unbreakable parting male shot: 'I'll call you.' Essentially, you are always waiting: at the dance (by now a club or disco) you wait for them to approach you. Then once they've escorted you home or you've been out with them – and decide you like them – you wait for the call. I've grown up with this, of course, but in my early twenties I still can't quite accept it. Yet all this stratified behavioural code, had I only known it, was about to be turned upside down in less than a decade. More honest, open exchanges between the sexes were on their way.

The one thing the 20-something '60s office girls have as their defence is their spending power on the latest fashionable gear. Traditional West End department stores like Swan and Edgar, Dickins & Jones and the new, fashionable chains like Neatawear go all out to tempt the young working spender with the very latest styles and fashions at prices aimed craftily at weekly pay packets. Temp secretaries, in particular, earn big sums working for an employment agency, moving around from office to office, if they're prepared to put up with the hassle of switching around to strange faces and bosses every few weeks. Many dislike this idea, even with the lure of more money.

I earn around £12 a week. I manage to supplement that for the year or so when I work at the electronics company by handing out good leads that have come direct to me, the sales manager's secretary, to a few select salesmen, getting £30 per sale in return. So I have plenty of cash to splash out on clothes, makeup and shoes. In fact, I blow the lot on clothes nearly every Friday when I receive my £9 (after deductions) pay packet, in exchange for my favourite styles: five guinea crepe dresses by Radley with wide trumpet sleeves or slinky, short, body-skimming shift dresses to go with tight, elasticated, white high boots from Dolcis, (£3 9 shillings and 11 pence) or killer pointy stilettos also costing a few pounds. What more does a girl need to get out there and attract?

Once the accounts girl has handed you the little brown envelope with the printed slip inside – no cash machines then or automatic salary transfers into a bank account, though 1966 saw the launch of the plastic revolution with the Barclaycard, the first credit card – away we all went at lunchtime, click-clicking down Oxford or Regent Street to a tiny Wallis (long relocated from its original home next to Oxford Circus tube, and still a popular chain to this day) or the bigger, pricier Fifth Avenue (long gone) on Regent Street or into one of the new boutiques for women popping up all around the hub of men's trendy gear shopping: Carnaby Street.

There are '60s labels I lust after like Tuffin and Foale (as spotted on Cathy McGowan on *Ready Steady Go*) and Cacharel from Paris. But they remain out of my price range, alas. Lured by the newspaper and *Honey* magazine hype, I venture to the famous Biba in its early days in Abingdon Road, off Kensington High Street one weekend. But the clothes in the packed little shop are far too tiny, cut too narrowly, too tight-sleeved and aimed at very lean King's Road girls. The smocks and the dyed skinny vests are for the flat-chested, not for me.

Yet once I do find what suits me elsewhere, a swift wriggle into the new ultra-short op-art dress, zip it up, add a pair of pale tights, low-cut patent shoes and lo! Instant transformation into the siren I hoped to be, complete with super-thick false eyelashes or carefully painted-on lower lashes, (thanks, Twiggy) pink Max

Factor lipstick, and a blonde, shoulder-length flick-up hairdo. And, of course, a small, quilted Chanel-style bag on a gold chain slung over the shoulder. The '60s look.

Of course, we can't all look like the high priestesses of classic mini-skirted '60s blonde. Women such as Patti Boyd, Julie Christie, Catherine Deneuve or Bardot (my secret role models – talk about aiming high. In this at least I have real ambition). I'm not lean enough to be a classic dolly bird, though the slinky, short, patterned dresses in man-made slippery fabrics suit my curvy shape. With an unruly, curly brown mop I am very far from the requisite natural blonde with straight, shiny hair. Somehow, I've managed to transform myself into a yellowish peroxide blonde, often with nasty dark roots. But the fashions of the time help: bad hair days can be disguised because all kinds of head gear and caps have become ultra-fashionable, especially the plastic pillbox hat, worn on the back of the head revealing only a dead straight fringe. Consider Mandy Rice Davies wearing such a hat outside the court in 1963 at the height of the Profumo affair. The hat covers a multitude of sins, if you'll forgive the pun.

Look carefully at those '60s photos of the commuters streaming down Waterloo Bridge to work or thronging Oxford Street or Piccadilly. You can't see too many overweight people, can you? My colleagues and girlfriends are different shapes and sizes – yet hardly any are what could be described as glaringly obese. The post-war generation, reared on free milk and NHS sticky orange juice as toddlers, remain quite lean by today's standards. Yet by today's standards, we eat badly – our office girl lunches, purchased with luncheon vouchers, now obligatory for any employer wishing to attract office staff, consist of cheese or ham crispy white rolls, Smith's crisps, Kit Kats, Lyon's Maid choc-ices or the somewhat dubious three-course café lunches for 2 shillings and 6 pence (watery tinned soup, something vaguely resembling meat and chips, treacle pudding and sticky yellow custard). All this, of course, is way too starchy and fat-laden. We are mostly ignorant about what really constitutes a sensible, healthy diet.

I've been diving into adventurous foreign eating territory in Soho, with cheap Chinese dishes like sweet'n'sour pork around Chinatown and Shaftesbury Avenue, since my late teens. Or sampling poppadums and curried chicken in north London Indian restaurants on my nights out with Bryan. But young women probably stay slim-ish because there aren't many fast food outlets around yet. Small workers' cafés, run by cheerful, hard-working Italian immigrant families, are the norm at lunchtime in the West End or the City, alongside the fast-growing rash of Wimpy Bars and Golden Egg chains spreading everywhere. These would eventually destroy places such as Lyons Corner Houses, so beloved of our parents' generation yet losing popularity all the time until their demise in the early 1970s. Pub food? This barely existed beyond the odd sandwich, scotch egg or ham roll. White bread only. ('Don't say brown, say Hovis' ran the 1950s ads for wheatgerm bread, but most pub managers continued to ignore anything but soggy sliced white bread well into the 1970s – and beyond).

In flesh-revealing terms, slimmer '60s women were pretty modest by today's standards. The mini is rampant, certainly, a revolutionary expression of new freedoms. There is a lot of leg and thigh on display. But you're unlikely to see a seven-month pregnant woman at a bus stop in a clingy outfit emphasising the bump. Modesty, even with the mini around, would not vanish overnight.

Parents are mostly horrified and somewhat puzzled at the exuberant rise of the show-all mini. 'You *can't* go out like that' becomes the mantra of a generation of women accustomed to 'making do' and rationing, using a black crayon to draw a fake 'seam' down the backs of their legs in wartime, nylon stockings having been virtually unavailable for many years. Now, those prized, precious, seamed nylons and suspender belts are on the way out too, replaced by the shiny white tights. Or, later, striped high socks with square-toed patent flats. It's truly daft to attempt to combine a mini with stockings and suspenders, though there's always the odd aberration, much to the delight of all the men in the office.

In a way, central London is my playground. I've grown up in a tough, streetwise area around Ridley Road market, but since my teens I've been spending most of my time working and going out in the West End, with occasional brief forays to fashionable Chelsea and Kensington. So the fashion influences are all around me, in my face, the shops a daily temptation. As a secretary I can job hop with remarkable impunity, mainly because there are so many office jobs on offer – and I am very easily bored. Offices big and small are taking on huge numbers of young school leavers and 20-somethings. With a bit of secretarial experience behind you, you can pick and choose, swapping around as often as you like.

For someone like me, with a restless, impatient nature, I am truly fortunate in that I hit the working world at just the right time: jobs a-go-go. Though with the carelessness of youth, I simply take this kind of freedom for granted. Gratitude for being given a job? Excuse me? Isn't it the other way round?

What I really hanker for, but never acknowledge, is some sort of challenge or stimulus in my daily trek to the typewriter. The day-to-day routine, waiting for men to dictate to you so you can type, spells stultifying boredom to me, only enlivened by banter and cheeky retorts to colleagues around the office and the contemplation of the after-work drink or that night's diversion. Yet such is the *laissez faire* of the employers, the ease with which office jobs are dished out, often with a minimum of formality (a CV was unknown, though a typed 'reference' from a previous job might be required by a diligent employer), I do manage to find the occasional minor challenge, simply because I opt to move around the job market frequently.

Far from being a model employee, the somewhat defiant, 'couldn't give a stuff' attitude I'd deployed at school has now morphed into a kind of sneery arrogance about it all. I'll do the work, rattle through it, no problem. I prefer to be doing, rather than just sitting around – something many bosses, who are quite happy to let you sit there twiddling your thumbs for much of the time, don't quite comprehend. But the whole package, the office location, the general environment, the ambience of the place has to suit me. Otherwise I'm off.

My attitude is best illustrated by a job I held for a while after I'd quit the electronics company following a swift and unexpected management change – and the booting out of my boss. For about 18 months afterwards I worked in a job that was on the fringes of London's '60s fashion explosion. Though you'd never have guessed it if you turned up at the rundown building tucked away in the mews behind Oxford Street where the company had its headquarters. Scruffy is a polite word to describe the exterior. Dead rodents, rubbish, torn boxes and birdshit greet the visitor. Without any health and safety laws or human resources policies to keep things in check, small companies frequently operated in less than healthy environments. Yet this job, with all its drawbacks, remains one of the more diverting – and memorable – ways I found to make a living in the late 1960s.

Essentially, the job involved a bizarre corporate cover-up. I was hired as a sort of personal assistant to a director of a chain of shoe stores. No one ever bothered to explain to me beforehand that the job mostly involved pretending to be a man. A man who did not exist. OK, it didn't go as far as me donning men's clothes or doing impersonations. But essentially, for the time I worked in those dingy offices, I and I alone acted as a man of power and influence within the company, signing letters and documents bearing his name and often pretending to be a direct conduit to this non-existent individual. I have his ear. I am his official right hand, as far as the customers are concerned. His name: Mr Kirk-Watson.

To this day, I have no idea if this man ever existed. All attempts to grill my boss and other colleagues about The Real Kirk-Watson lead nowhere. No one ever actually knew him or anything about him. But in the minds of the shoe chain's many customers, he is a significant presence indeed. And for the endlessly harassed store managers — the fast-expanding chain consists of about a dozen shops, all under consistent pressure to sell, sell, sell the fashionable shoes — he is their sole backup. Because Mr Kirk-Watson is effectively, a one-man customer service bureau, the person to whom all serious complaints about the shoes, mostly imported from Italy, are to be directed if the store manager cannot satisfy a complainant on the spot.

'Madam, I'm sorry but I will have to refer you to Mr Kirk-Watson at head office,' the manager would say ruefully, offering the often irate customer my office phone number before they stomped out of the store, muttering all sorts of threats involving the police, their family, the newspapers and so on. (TV consumer programmes such as the BBC's *Watchdog* didn't surface until the 1980s.) Consumer power – and legislation to protect the consumer – has not yet arrived.

Let me explain exactly why the customer frequently – and justifiably – loses the plot. The problem is that at a time when young, fashion-conscious customers with cash to spend are being courted like crazy, some retail outfits, focusing on turnover rather than quality or customer service, do not see themselves as being under any serious obligation to offer cash refunds if the goods are not up to scratch for some reason (and often they're not, being produced in a mad rush to cash in quickly). Nor is there any widespread public knowledge showing, quite clearly, what the deal should be – what the retailer is legally obliged to offer the customer if the goods are undeniably faulty.

As for the shoes, usually at the cutting edge of fashion – stiletto heels with pointy toes, Chelsea or thigh-high boots, flat shoes with amazing trims – they are, as now, priced to tempt the weekly pay packets of the office girls and boys thronging Oxford Street and the surrounding shopping streets of central London. Yet these shoes are sometimes badly made. Heels fall off after one or two wearings. Sole and upper sometimes come apart within days. Trims or buckles just drop off.

The company import these shoes because they're both ultra-fashionable and carry an extremely high profit mark-up. In Italy, still struggling to get its post-war export markets going, labour is much cheaper than here. So head office decree that the inconvenient issue of shoddy workmanship and angry customers is one for store managers to resolve, primarily to the advantage of the company. With the help of a man who does not exist. Looking back, I suspect that the use of a double-barrelled name was an attempt to impose some sort of intimidation on the lower orders. If so, they got it wrong because, by the late 1960s, cap-doffing and knowing thy place is on the wane – especially in the West End, the epicentre of all change. Though the quaint domestic service habit, where the servant employee uses the prefix 'Mr' before the boss's first name ('Mr Jack') still prevails in this particular office.

In extremis, a credit note could be offered by the manager. Or even a replacement pair of shoes, if in stock. But shop managers, mostly, hold back from making these offers because credit notes affect their takings – and their commission. Head office policy ensures that they can hardly ever take any money out of the till and hand it back. The policy around complaints is to take the offending shoes back, offer to send them for repair and, if customers are still not happy with this, offer them Mr Kirk-Watson's number to get them out of the store. A really furious or persistent phone call to Mr Kirk-Watson might – just – result in a credit note being issued direct from head office and not affecting shop takings. But a cash refund? Not on your nelly.

So the real Mr Kirk-Watson – a mini-skirted, mouthy, peroxide blonde with back-combed, lacquered flick ups and serious attitude to all comers – spends much of the working day fending off the stream of Kirk-Watson phone calls from angry or disgruntled customers. Now and again, the odd customer might venture into the premises to confront the elusive man, but once directed to the grungy ground-floor entrance at the back of the building, the only target for their ire is a lone receptionist, a tough blonde from the far end of the Metropolitan line called Babs. I am three floors up, safe in my tiny cubbyhole off my boss's somewhat larger office. I never actually see a customer face to face.

My boss – Tom, the Oxbridge-educated son and heir to the booming business built up by his canny family in swift response to the ever-growing demand for fashionable gear for swingin' Londoners – is rarely there. Nor does he ask much from me if he is around. Skinny, abrupt and often strangely distracted – it's obvious that the demands of retailing are not really his thing, though I never discover what is – he is a timid sort of man, a weed really, in a crumpled three-piece suit that could easily have been slept in. It does not trouble me to take the endless stream of Kirk-Watson calls. The alternative is chatting to my friends on the phone or typing the odd bit of correspondence that, for some bizarre reason, Tom usually scribbles out for me in a disgusting scrawl – had he trained as a doctor? – on the back of old shoe boxes, a recycling habit he surely picked up from his mum during the war.

Tom's fiancé, Helene – a French glamour puss – occasionally wafts into head office, reeking of Arpège and smothered in expensive Jean Muir or sporting ultra-fashionable short, pricey Jean Varon dresses (the designer's real name was John Bates, the man who designed the clothes for the TV series *The Avengers*). Worldly and snobbish, she clearly overwhelms titchy Tom in every way. In her presence, he is a stuttering, gibbering wreck. An odd couple indeed. Tom has some strange habits. One involves light bulbs. When a new bulb goes in, he writes down the date. Then, when it pops, he carefully notes how long it lasted – a futile exercise as far as I could see, unless he planned to spend his life chasing Osram, the company making the bulbs. Letters are under careful surveillance too. If a letter misses the franking machine and needs a stamp, only second-class post may be used. And so on.

The Kirk-Watson scenario would at least prove to be good training for a future life as a journalist on the phone, talking to people who mostly don't really want to talk to you – or alternatively, have a particular axe to grind. My phone routine is to politely present myself as K-W's sidekick, explain that he's away in Italy on a shoe-buying trip and offer to hear out their complaint. (If the customer has flatly refused to have the offending shoes sent off for repair, they are sometimes sent round to head office by the store manager, who phones me in advance to warn of an impending super-stroppy caller.) I have one available option (which rarely works) and politely offer to have the shoes sent off to the official body governing Britain's shoe trade if the customer is willing to wait for a third-party decision on their complaint. This they mostly reject. So as a final resort, in what is clearly a hopeless case, I am empowered to offer a credit note – but usually after consultation with Tom and/or a manager.

Tom never argues or queries it when I put a credit note request in front of him. He lets me authorise and sign them, as Mr Kirk-Watson, in his frequent absences. With my East End background, acutely aware of fiddle potential, I could have expanded my personal shoe wardrobe considerably this way. Yet I don't give in to this particular temptation, not because of any inherent scruple, but because it seems too easy to bother with and anyway, I get a good staff discount. As for Tom, he just wants a quiet life. After all, I'm taking the crap from a daily stream of angry customers who are mostly justified in thinking they're getting a rotten, totally unfair deal.

The shoe trade body do their bit, examining the shoes sent to them, explaining what has gone wrong in a polite letter, offering the customer a repair plus further advice on looking after their shoes. But of course, most customers don't want this somewhat protracted deal, which takes weeks. They want their hard-earned cash back. Now.

And so I get used to people yelling at me, threatening to expose my company's underhand ways, calling me a variety of unpleasant names because they can't get their money back. Mostly I can't reason with them (there is, of course, no training whatsoever for my customer service role, no direction on how to handle the unhappy customer), so I devise a neat trick. If the yelling and abuse goes on – and sometimes it continues for a few minutes, which is a real time-waster – I simply get on with my work, type my letters, carefully placing the phone beside me in the top drawer of my desk. That way I let the yelling, screaming customer give vent to their feelings without the irresistible temptation of answering them back or telling them to 'eff off. It gets a tad repetitive being told for the umpteenth time what a bitch I am, that my boss is a criminal, my employers thieves who deserve a good thumping. I discover a distinct pattern to their abuse. For once they've exhausted their vocabulary, run out of epithets, they frequently stop – and just slam the phone down in disgust.

So there I sit, a one-woman call centre with a timid

boss and a rather odd game of passing the buck. It's the lively, hyped-up shop managers, mostly, who keep me in stitches when we phone each other about the worst of it: the husband who pleads with us to refund the money because he's so terrified of his wife's vitriol, the screaming mum whose teenage daughter is in floods of tears because she wanted to wear the new stilettos on Saturday night, the posh woman who believes it's her right to order 'you shop people' around and who claims all sorts of political connections with Churchill's family to get her £10 back.

So there they all are, frustrated consumers in a world where there are no other means of redress other than firing their verbal bullets down a big black Bakelite phone on an unsteady wooden desk. And a 20-something girl in a thigh-high dress who doesn't give a toss, feet up on the desk, as the frustrated customer screams themselves hoarse. Into an empty drawer.

CHAPTER TWO

A SECRET TRIP
ON THE
CENTRAL LINE

I am facing a shocking moment of truth. There is no escape from this. I have been stupid, careless and, typically, blindly convinced that it couldn't possibly happen to me.

But right now, in this miserable, freezing cold surgery, with its slippery vinyl couch upon which I have just been probed, eyes glued firmly to the cracked grey ceiling, small fists clenched more in anger than fear, I am stunned into silence by the doctor's words. And he isn't bothering to be kind. Or sensitive. Why should he? I'm an unmarried young woman who has fallen into an old trap: I am pregnant. A heated, immensely pleasurable but nonetheless speedy exchange of bodily fluids, deshabille, on the rear seat of a parked car near Haverstock Hill, has led me here. Into the pudding club. Many women

29

dream of this moment, this amazing discovery of the creation of life. But some don't.

'You're probably about eight weeks gone,' Dr King says, coldly, not even bothering to look at me as he scribbles on the beige card in front of him. I have come here, to the NHS GP's surgery in Dalston, a 22-year-old who doesn't know where to run, what to do. I left home many months before. But officially, I'm still on King's 'panel' because I haven't bothered to sort out a doctor near my new flat. In 1967, despite all the brouhaha around the 'permissive society' there were no over-the-counter pregnancy tests available, purchased from Boots, to conduct in privacy. If you missed one or two periods, your breasts started to swell and you felt overwhelmed by lassitude in the middle of the day, there was only one route ahead for confirming what your body was already telling you: the NHS GP. And mine, while a respected man in the area, is no moderniser. He's not on side with the politicians already looking ahead to actually changing the draconian laws that made pregnancy termination or abortion an illegal and often dangerous practice for women.

In fact, King is very much a religious man, born in regimented Edwardian days when the very worst that could befall a young unmarried woman was pregnancy: whatever the circumstances, even rape, society insisted then that the man was never ever culpable, held to account. A child born out of wedlock was a complete no-no. To this man, I'm a fallen woman, a social disgrace. 'You can make arrangements for adoption,' he tells me. 'There's plenty of Jewish families wanting to adopt.' I stare at him. He stares back, the iceman. To him, I'm a just an irresponsible girl, all the stuff the papers allude to in the dawning of flower power and psychedelia. We might be reading about it all, yet such fantastic American notions as 'Make love, not war' haven't yet made it across the pond to Dalston. Nor are these ideas likely to affect this man's beliefs.

If he could, I think fleetingly, he'd probably throw me out. My parents, like so many older people who thank their lucky stars for the still relatively new NHS, think he's God, not King. Until today, even I thought he was OK, old fashioned but… he knew his job. 'But… there *must* be something I can do,' I plead. 'I can't have a baby, I can't.'

Even now, in the midst of my turmoil, what he's suggesting about adoption is anathema to me. I just don't want to have a baby. Full stop. Go through with it? He must be crazy. Yet at this point in time, he's my only hope in the world: this grim, ageing figure of rigid authority in his stiff, three-piece suit, the remnants of his dark wavy hair plastered carefully to one side, his hateful rubber gloves now lying in a steel bowl on a side table. I detest him, his judgement from on high, his power over everyone round here. Yet he and he alone has the knowledge, the power to help me. I ask him again, what can I *do*? 'No. There's nothing,' he says, his words clipped and curt. 'Girls like you should be grateful for whatever help you get when you have the baby. You can to go to the hospital and get it all checked out in two weeks time.' More furious scribbling on the beige card.

He doesn't say, 'Get out now.' But his body language as he continues to write, ignoring my presence, nudges me to leave. So I teeter out in my brown pointy stilettos, through the packed surgery, past the wailing Bash Street kids of Dalston, out on to the grey, ever-depressing world of Sandringham Road, its once proud and splendid Victorian family houses now derelict and war-ravaged, crammed with immigrant West Indian families dreaming of the balmy Caribbean world and the happy life they've left behind – having reached the revered mother country only to be ripped off outrageously by greedy, uncaring landlords. And treated like pariahs by most of the population round here.

My parents' flat is just up the road. But there's no way I'm going there. I've taken the day off work to do this, see the doctor. They'd ask questions if I turned up mid-week. Instead, I walk in the opposite direction towards Ridley Road market, thinking hard, pushing myself to come up with something, anything that will help get me out of this situation. I've told no one at all about what I fear is happening to me, not my flatmates, who are provincial, middle-class girls in London to work and find husbands, nor the man who got me here, my new squeeze from the office, the gregarious Jeff. Jeff is a bit of a secret lover, anyway. No one knows I'm sleeping with him. The girls in the flat and my friends know about my on-off (mostly off) boyfriend, Bryan, the adman. He's still an Official Boyfriend. But that's it. What a mess.

Then, at the junction of Ridley and Sandringham Roads, where you encounter the market itself, the rickety stalls, the slimy, mucky muddle of urban street trading, I remember a conversation I had ages ago, with an old friend from Hackney schooldays, Doreen, a girl I rarely see now since I've moved to a different world in north-west London. The connection with my old life, growing up here, these familiar streets, opens up a flash of hope. Yes. Doreen. She knows someone. She told me all about it over the phone. This happened to her. But her boyfriend's uncle knew someone and her boyfriend, a wealthy foreign student, paid for it all. It was fine. Oh, how lucky I am that troubled day. Salvation is merely round the corner. Doreen, a tiny, skinny girl with a curly short crop, lives in an old block of flats in Dalston Lane with her dad and her younger brother. She's had a rotten deal. Her mum died when Doreen was small, so she's more or less had to bring up her younger brother and look after her dad, who is now quite old. Education never featured large in Doreen's life and she doesn't work, apart from occasional part-time hours in a high street dress shop.

She's home, cheerfully offering me a cup of lemon tea

and a rich tea biscuit in the cluttered front room of their cramped flat. Her dad remains, as ever, inert in the bedroom. I give her a brief version of events. Does she still know that man? Does she still have the number? Yes, she's got it. 'But it costs about £80,' she warns me. 'How you gonna pay for it?'

'I'll find a way,' I tell her, carefully writing the number down. It means deception of the worst order. But I've already come up with an idea about getting the money for an abortion – way beyond my own resources since I never save a penny out of what I earn.

The next night, when the flat I share with the three other girls is temporarily deserted, I dial the number from the coin box in our hallway. Push button A. A man with a foreign accent answers. I don't beat around the bush. 'I'm pregnant and I don't want it. My friend says you can help me,' I say boldly. I'm not in the least bit embarrassed about all this. I want what I want: to get out of this fast – and I'm told this man can do it. But I don't know a thing about him. I don't even know if he is a doctor. As usual, I'm not interested in detail. Can he help? Silence. This is still illegal, dodgy, no question. We both know that. He chooses his words carefully, an obvious Eastern European accent. But his English is quite good.

'Yes, we can help. Bring the money with you when you come for the appointment. How many weeks?' He doesn't use the word 'pregnant' at all. I explain, briefly, what I know, tell him I've seen a GP. 'That is good. We are in Ealing. Can you come next Wednesday? Ring again tomorrow, we give you a time.'

And that's it. A week away. The next bit, getting the money, is going to be really fraught. There's not much trepidation involved in ringing up a total stranger, asking them to carry out a highly dangerous and illegal operation in their home. But I am very nervous, edgy, about what my next move involves. Because I must lie through my teeth. It's about two months or more since I have slept with Bryan. But my decision has been made: I know the timing. I keep a diary of my period dates and it's definitely Jeff who is the dad, not Bryan. Jeff will be told about all this. But only once it's over, sorted. Passion overwhelmed me that night in the car, our first time, risky business indeed. Yet Bryan is another matter: a man who has been having his cake and eating it (if you'll forgive the expression) for a long time. OK, it was my decision to stick around, still see him on the odd occasion whenever he felt like it. But now, I reason, with his Official Boyfriend status, Bryan can fork out. So I dial his number.

'Jesus-fucking-Christ, I thought you were on the bloody pill,' is his response.

I had managed to get a prescription via a Family Planning Association clinic back when Bryan and I were a proper item, seeing each other regularly. But I'd hated taking it – it made me feel sick. So after a few months I stopped. And then we'd lapsed into our on-off state, with big gaps of several weeks between our dates. The last time we slept together in his posh flat, with Donovan serenading us with 'Sunshine Superman' on the Dansette, Bryan was quite drunk and ignored my admittedly half-hearted suggestion of 'using something' .So I'm pretty sure he doesn't really remember much about the night at all, let alone when it was. He's not going to be counting weeks or consulting the calendar. He doesn't really know for sure, I tell myself. And I'm right. Bryan doesn't bother to calculate. All he wants is instant resolution. 'OK, so what do you wanna do? Oh, you've got someone. Good. How much?' he says warily. He knows me well enough to know that I'm not going to even suggest I have this baby, keep it.

I tell all him about Ealing, the price, the appointment.

'Right. I'll drop round Friday night and give you the money.' Click.

The odd thing is, even though I'm lying to him, I'm really upset at his lack of concern. Daft, eh? By now, with the changes taking place already in my body, my hormones are all over the place, so I'm bound to feel wildly irrational. Yet my anguish at his indifference gets worse when he turns up that Friday. I've been hanging out the window for ages, waiting for him, so I run down to the front door when I hear his souped-up Mini. No, he can't come up, he's in a hurry. He just hands me the money, all £10 notes for some reason. 'I'll ring you,' he says coldly, his usual parting shot. Then he screeches off. Typical.

'He's a bastard,' I tell myself for the umpteenth time as I climb the stairs to my bedroom, clutching the notes. 'He deserves this,' I say over and over again. Yet it still feels lousy, a betrayal of sorts. But logic dictates that I can't afford the emotional luxury of spending time on reflection, right or wrong, in this situation. I've acted out of sheer expedience. Bryan has cash, I don't. And I do not want to stay pregnant. Simple. Even so, I spend the next few days in a pretty miserable state. If ever I needed confirmation that Bryan was a callous shit, this is it.

The following Wednesday, I call in sick at work and make my way on the Central line to Ealing Broadway. Then I walk, following the man's carefully dictated instructions, for about ten minutes to a big Edwardian house, where I ring the big white bell for the ground floor flat. I'm not nervous, shaking, tearful or anything like that. I'm glad no one is with me. The distraction wouldn't have helped me. My mind is holding fast to what I want to achieve. I cannot – will not – let fear or any other emotion creep in. It's bad enough when I think about Bryan the Bastard.

It's a big, spacious, spotless, high-ceilinged hallway that I'm asked to sit in, briefly, by a youngish woman who answers the door before an older, smiling blonde woman in a blue overall comes out to greet me. She's a big round lady, about 35, well-groomed, lacquered, bouffant hair, manicured nails. Smart but at the same time motherly. She also has a foreign accent. Yet she exudes a low-key confidence, a professionalism that is somehow reassuring. She ushers me into a very large area, part-office, part-surgery where the man is sitting waiting. He is much younger than Dr King, maybe late thirties, spotless white coat, good looking, sandy hair, also very pleasant. Perhaps they're a husband-wife team. He jumps up, greets me by name, shakes my hand, asks me for the money which I willingly dig out of my little Chanel-style padded shoulder bag, briefly noticing the big table in the centre of the room with its scary metal stirrups, something I've never seen before. Gulp. This is it.

Yet I don't baulk or falter as the woman shows me into a corner cubicle behind a flimsy screen, tells me to undress and put on a short thin robe. I am about to have an illegal abortion without a general anaesthetic. It is highly dangerous for so many reasons: prosecution and prison face people like these if they are apprehended. Girls like me face even greater dangers if something goes wrong, if non-sterile instruments or incorrect procedures are used – or if a body goes into shock at undergoing such a process while wide awake. You might bleed to death afterwards and die. Today, if placed in such a situation, I'd be absolutely terrified, shaking, practically hysterical. It would probably be nigh impossible to treat me. I'm well aware of the complexities of the human body, the possibilities of what might happen at the hands of an inefficient practitioner. Today, I don't trust most doctors unless I have real confidence in their manner, their skills. I am acutely nervous of all forms of physical intervention. Even a visit to the dentist is something to be avoided.

Oh, the invincibility of youth! No true sense of your own mortality, your human frailty. The young do ridiculously stupid, reckless things because they have no anticipation of pain. So that day, in that big room in Ealing, I blindly place myself at the mercy of these two individuals, an eastern European couple whom I later understand must have fled their own country and Communism after the political upheavals of the 1950s. He's probably a qualified doctor there, but how he has arrived at this situation, dodging the law and risking much, is open to question. Probably this is a better bet than the alternative: a life without freedom behind the grim iron curtain.

I obediently do what I'm told – get up on the table, submit to the awful stirrups. There is no bad, wrenching pain, just acute discomfort which is endurable when I look away, stare at anything, rather than acknowledge the reality of the cold surgical instruments, the procedure itself. There's a brief, jolting, sharp injection, a local anaesthetic before it all starts. The woman is amazingly professional, quietly chatting to me, asking me questions about my life, distracting my thoughts from what the doctor is doing to my body. I know it's all going just fine because she keeps reminding me, briefly, in that soothing way of practised, caring medics. Until, after about 20 or so minutes, though it could well have been longer, the man is telling me, 'It's OK. Nearly over.' Then, a few minutes later: 'You're not pregnant any more.' How well he understood it all.

This couple, whatever their story, are knowledgeable and confident. After I've stepped down somewhat shakily from the table, dressed and been handed a cup of something warm, the man hands me some painkillers – which I never take – and explains what to do when I get home and what to expect (which proves to be nothing dramatic). He also tells me to ensure I have a cervical smear test done every year, something I've never heard of before. 'You must do this test each year, just in case there are any problems,' he explains. He doesn't use the word 'cancer'. Such information is not widely understood by women at this time: newspapers and magazines give out some information on health and medicine, but it's nothing like the plethora of detail and useful, valuable advice on every topic under the sun that we can access today. Or the abundance of shock-horror, 'This could be happening to you,' scary detail we are also exposed to now.

I nod, grateful, relieved beyond belief that it is done. I'm out of trouble. I've got through this. My life can go on as before. Then he offers to drive me back to north London. He ushers me into the back seat of his dark-blue Jaguar, which would have cost around £1,800 then. The average worker in the mid-1960s lived on around £1,200 a year. This was surely a lucrative business.

At the end of that same year, 1967, the abortion bill passes through Parliament, making it legal in the UK for up to 28 weeks gestation. The Act comes into effect in April 1968. Abortion, by a registered practitioner, then becomes free in England via the NHS. Perhaps people such as the clued-up couple knew this was coming and so took ever-greater risks while they could. There would have been plenty of demand for their unadvertised services, though the £80 might have been a stumbling block for many, given the average wage packet.

How do I feel afterwards? Pretty shaky. Though there are no dramatic physical after-effects. No one in the flat knows my secret – my trip down the Central line – and I haven't told my mother, Molly. Yet emotionally, of course, I am not in a good place: weepy for weeks, strangely quiet, no interest at all in forays to the clubs of the West End, dancing, being chatted up. I have some sort of post-termination blues. Consciously, I do not want a baby. Ever. But my hormones, over which I have no control, have been gearing up for a different story.

Perhaps because of this, I'm still emotionally fixated on Bryan, even though I know this drama and my duplicity presages the end of whatever relationship we have. Pretty tragic, really. He does ring briefly after a day or so, just to check I'm OK. But he doesn't ask to see me, though I'm vulnerable enough to utter those pathetic words: 'But when will I *see* you…?' Nah. Too busy. Going abroad for work. Will call. That call does not come.

I do tell Jeff exactly what has happened. The look on his face – sheer relief he hasn't even been required to get remotely involved – says it all. He's had a blindingly lucky escape. Had I been a different sort of girl, one who wants a baby, married or not, he'd have been in a right pickle. (The more I know Jeff, the more the details of his complicated private life puzzle yet elude me: I do not yet know he already has one illegitimate child. That he never sees. So he must have been exceptionally thankful that it hadn't happened again.) He's been irresponsible, but so have I, juggling two boyfriends in this way. My view is: I can't really blame him for all this. He represents fun, laughter – and hot sex. But the thing is, I've known Bryan the Bastard over quite a long period of time. My attachment to him is born of familiarity. He wasn't the first lover, technically speaking. But he was the first man I'd had sex with on a regular basis. Emotionally, there was bound to be some sort of attachment.

After a few months, I'm more or less back to my normal self. And I start to understand how different Jeff is from my previous lover, simply because he's so much more skilled in bed. I'm an all too willing pupil, though he's very consistent when it comes to using condoms. Bryan wasn't even in the same league as Jeff, who knows by a combination of strong instinct and experience what turns a woman on. Foreplay, beyond the initial lunge for my bra strap and a swift nibble, was a waste of time to Bryan (not that he's alone in this, as I will discover in time). And he always needed booze or marijuana before sex.

His ad agency world of top-level contacts did give him access to the exclusive, inner circle of swinging London. He hung out in trendy places where the Beatles went, such as the Ad Lib Club in Leicester Square (though he never took me). Or frequented tiny exclusive clubs like the Scotch of St James or The Bag (The Bag O'Nails in Kingly Street, where, legend has it, Linda first hooked Beatle Paul). Once, in the very early days of our affair, Bryan escorted me to a party in an enormous, totally intimidating house in its own grounds in grandest Surrey, where Charlie Watts of the Stones was a revered if somewhat silent guest. At the time, I was both wildly impressed and totally overawed at Bryan's connections. But that one-off party made it very clear to me: Bryan kept his worlds in totally separate compartments.

Jeff – much better-looking, 6ft 2ins tall, blond hair, hard muscled body, oozing sexual charisma – is a far less sophisticated man, quite working class. Think Michael Caine as the chauffeur lothario in *Alfie* – the movie of 1966 that daringly highlighted the emerging sexual freedoms of the era and the whole abortion dilemma in a scary way never seen on screen before – and you'd be fairly close to Jeff's style. He's more a quick half in the pub, 1/6d pie and chips man, suits from Austin Reed (purchased on an HP account), £5 a week, not much of a drinker, more of an action man, in his mind at least. He sees himself clearly in bold letters 'A Man Born to Shag as Many Women as Possible'.

At this point I haven't quite worked it all out, though soon I will see everything more clearly. Eventually, the whole post-abortion emotional mess in my head starts to recede. With hindsight, I was incredibly resilient. Of course, I didn't manage to brush it all off completely. I wasn't that insensitive nor was I in any doubt that I'd deployed deceit of a questionable order. So any guilt I felt was around that, not around ending the pregnancy. But you do tend to bounce back quite quickly at that stage of life, especially if your personal default setting is not to take on responsibility – of any kind.

Funnily enough, Jeff always got slightly ratty at the merest mention of Bryan. I worked out that this had nothing to do with any real jealousy around me, you understand. More a bit of a class thing. Bryan had been privately educated, easing him into a really good job in ad-land. Jeff's status, though he kidded himself otherwise, was more of Cockney chancer. Car ownership constantly troubled Jeff too, a typically male perspective. Bryan whizzed around swingin' London either in the Mini, a present from his doting dad, or a newly acquired adman's sports car, a gleaming red TR4. Compare that to Jeff's much-prized company car, the Rover, which he banged on about ad nauseum yet could never afford himself. Yet which one could really lay claim to having the biggest and best appendage?

'It's not the size of your knob, it's what you do with it,' was one of Bryan's favourite quips. Perhaps this was a reassuring statement for a man who knew damn well he wasn't generously endowed. But as I was starting to realise as I found out much more about the 'what you do with it' bit, the art of self-deception knows no bounds whatsoever when it comes to the fragile male ego.

CHAPTER THREE

RANDY SANDY AND THE CHICKENS

A lone envelope lies on the mat. Still half-awake, I stumble bleary-eyed down the stairs from my bedroom the minute I hear the rat-tat of the letterbox. It's Saturday and I've been anticipating this all week: the missive that will redirect the course of my life. For ever. Yes, it's addressed to me. As I pick it up, even before I open it, I can see by the bold markings on the thick white envelope that this is it: the Big Plan is about to bear fruit. Until this moment, it has remained just an idea – someone else's idea, at that.

Somewhat recklessly, I've agreed to go along with it. Why not? I'm free, white and 21 (an American saying never heard now, for obvious reasons, but one often used then). On the surface, at least, the plan is immensely appealing, adventurous, more exciting than anything I've ever come up with. Yet in my usual slapdash fashion, I have not really thought it all through, gone into it in depth or given it sensible, serious consideration. Leaving me totally unprepared for what it all really means now that I've reached the final hurdle…

'It's a bloody daft idea, Jacky,' Jeff had sneered that early spring evening a few months before when I'd outlined The Plan to him as we sat drinking outside the Bull and Bush, a handy local mainly because you could sit outside (al fresco eating and drinking in London was very much a novelty then, at a time when people could smoke themselves silly indoors in pubs and restaurants with no complaints at all about the accompanying unhealthy haze). 'You don't wanna go and do that, gorgeous – what about me?' he smiles, lighting up his usual Churchmans cigarella (five shillings and tuppence for a pack of 20) to accompany his occasional bottle of Double Diamond ('works wonders,' said the advert, though what kind of wonders remained vague; for most men it was surely the hope of a swift leg-over after closing time). 'Are you saying you can really live without me?'

'Yeah, I can live without you. Don't kid yourself,' I tell him tartly. I'm not that surprised he's shown no enthusiasm for The Plan. But his attitude isn't exactly helpful. Nor does it help when he drops me off at my flat that night with a lingering kiss that leaves me weak-kneed, wet-knickered and hungry for the following weekend's promise: conjugal bliss in his friend's tiny cottage in Kent. He's blinding me with sex, I sigh to myself as I totter on my perilous Dolcis stilettos down the dark alleyway to my front door: he thinks I'm not really going to go through with it.

It's funny, isn't it? Here is Jeff, a regular if somewhat erratic fixture in my world, questioning my idea to really get out there and do something different with my life – even while there remain a number of big unanswered questions hanging over our relationship, the main one being is he really faithful, never mind, where does he really live?

We're no longer working in the same sales office where we'd met. As a consequence, we see less of each other. Yes, he takes me on weekend jaunts: onto a friend's yacht (I loathe every minute of it, cold, wet and at one point quite scary when we have to abandon ship and climb up a perilously narrow ladder on a harbour wall to safety). Or to motor race meetings in various parts of the country. Sometimes, on his sales trips, we drive north on the brand new M1, the UK's first motorway, linking south to north via the Midlands. This means we couple up as Mr and Mrs Jeff in seedy provincial hotels. There's a frisson of the forbidden, the sleazy, about such trips and while my taste for luxury and comfort has yet to be fine-tuned, I find this all exciting, a turn-on, if I'm completely honest.

He's an ongoing stimulus, is Jeff. I have the serious hots for him, no question. Yet somehow, whenever I express a doubt about him or ask a pertinent question, he always manages to head me off with a sexy or romantic gesture. And it's always exactly the right one to throw me off balance, shut me up. He's pitch-perfect at seduction, flatters outrageously, woos me beautifully (which means I find myself believing what he's saying – at the time). Jeff is constantly telling me how gorgeous I am, how he loves my legs, adores my figure, and so on. He comes from a tough background. As a girl and an only child I was over-protected by my indulgent parents, shielded from the worst of the mean streets of Hackney. Jeff was one of three kids in a tiny cottage with a tough father who worked erratically and a mother who worked in a laundry. Yet Jeff knows and understands the value of the spoken word, the seductively pitched voice when it comes to the lists of love. Even from a distance, he uses the phone seductively.

Nowadays women can make a good living from just sitting at home, getting paid to talk men into orgasmic heaven on the mobile while cleaning out the kitchen cupboard at the same time. Everybody wins. Yet in the '60s, before sex evolved into a packaged commodity for all comers, it was the guys who understood the subtleties of the chase – like deploying a smoothly sensual voice down the phone line – that frequently had the edge when it came to success with many women. Remember that hot, steamy phone call from Michael Caine to Britt Ekland in the early 1970s movie *Get*

Carter? It was one of the first times Brit-style phone sex was openly celebrated on screen. ('Just doing my exercises, darling.') That was definitely a Jeff scenario.

Let's be clear. I am not lacking in romantic impulse at this point. I am thrilled to be wooed like this – it's so exciting. But at the same time, I don't believe myself to be so in love with Jeff that I envisage a rose-tinted future, us bonded together, welded fast in some sort of sticky permanence. It's never like that. It's very much an affair of the here and now. I love the excitement of it all. Yet I also know what kind of man he is around women because I've worked with him. I'd see it with my own eyes. Loverboy Jeff aims to flirt with or chat up many women because he sees something attractive or desirable in practically every woman that crosses his path – and he sees no reason to hide it. For him, it's all a joyful game.

This behaviour, of course, is not exactly reassuring. It's quite unnerving – it shakes my confidence. I give a good impression of a confident, streetwise girl, hiding my insecurities behind my short-skirted armour, a sarcastic tongue and a cynical demeanour. Yet I am no different to most of my gender emotionally. It rattles me to know he's appreciative of so many women in this way. But he's cleverly manipulative too, always tapping into to my main character weakness, my undisciplined laissez faire, easily persuading me to overcome my reservations about his outrageously flirtatious behaviour – and keep going along with him on the ride marked Destination: Pleasure.

And what pleasure it is. It's the beginning of what evolves into an intense attraction to sex as a hedonistic, recreational pursuit for me. It's all wonderfully unpredictable too. Sometimes it's urgent, passionate, speedy. But there are times when it's tantalisingly slow and sensual, depending on the location (sleazy hotel room versus the back of the Rover – my shared bedroom is a no-go most of the time). He flicks the switch, I react instantly. Away from him, I'm often swamped with sheer physical lust, wanting touch, smooth flesh on flesh so much it almost hurts. This is all totally new for me, an unknown country. As is the not inconsiderable discovery that Jeff can bring me to orgasm quite easily – something Bryan never achieved, probably because he was pretty much a one-speed lover. If you like, Bryan was my first course, a mere appetiser. Jeff was the complete menu. As many delicious, lip-smacking courses as a woman could stand.

Yet his life was a blank canvas. I don't have a home phone number for him and if I do ring his office, he's never there, according to the secretary who answers the phone. He claims it's his own business now, him and another guy 'selling insurance'. That's all I know. It's not a covert situation: he proudly shows me off to some of his friends sometimes – they're all a lot older than him, mostly established businessmen in their forties – and it's obvious too that in their eyes I'm a bit of a catch, a '60s babe with knockers. But there's no point in grilling any of them for guidance: they too are in on the act. Jeff's a very naughty boy, that's the underlying theme of their joshing and semi-lascivious, yet outwardly respectful glances at me around the pub bar. So how could I catch him out?

As for my life outside Jeff, sharing a flat with other girls has proved to be a big culture shock for me. Liberation from my dad and the grotty Dalston milieu had been easily achieved. I'd responded to a few newspaper ads and found a suitable locale, over a parade of shops fronting the Finchley Road. But now I was faced with day-to-day living with three other young women. And their underwear cluttering the place, their big, red hair rollers, their daily grooming rituals – hair in the sink and pubes in the bath, talcum powder all over the bathroom floor – and, on occasion, their trickle of eager suitors, mainly local guys in their twenties, eager for the promise of girl action. Now I am supposed to muck in, give room for others. It's called sharing – unknown terrain for a spoilt, solitary kid whose mum ran round her like a virtual slave. I have to fend for myself food-wise, wash my own clothes, maintain a semblance of tidiness in my quarters and so on. This, of course, is not so different from the way many youngsters are today when they first swap the comforts of the parental home for university and rented places. Except that today the landlord (or doting parents) might provide a labour-saving microwave, washing machine, even a dishwasher.

Such devices were then largely unknown in messy, shabby, rented flats. We didn't have a vacuum cleaner, just a little carpet sweeper that didn't really do the job. If you were lucky – and we were – we had a launderette close by. But even that meant the better part of an evening sitting there, waiting for the slow machines to do their job. Even the service wash hadn't reached the Finchley Road by then.

This flat was quaintly termed a 'maisonette' with rooms on two levels. You reached it by climbing crumbly stairs at the back of the shopping parade and then negotiating a quite dim, narrow passageway – and a jumble of rubbish – to reach the front doors leading directly to the flats above the shops. Inside, more stairs took you to a sparsely furnished, big living room and a greasy kitchen with a greyish lino-covered floor that was perpetually slippery but never clean, a bedroom and bathroom on the same level, then more narrow stairs (at the foot of which you encountered the landlord's thoughtful and all-important coin box phone) up to another lounge and a second bedroom right at the top. It was quite a spacious place, as flats above shops often are. But such was the demand for rented 'furnished' accommodation then, landlords didn't need to offer anything beyond the very basics.

Ancient green, moth-eaten velvet curtains, probably

pre-war, in the living rooms, permanently drawn to cover up the grimy, soot-stained windows that were never ever cleaned. Threadbare flooring (calling it carpet would be going too far), wobbly G-plan table and chairs (G-plan was the 1950s simple wood furniture which proliferated across the country for decades) and a heavily stained, dark green sofa made up this 'fully furnished' place. There was a 1950s TV, though it was rarely switched on and, somewhat surprisingly, a red Dansette record player, on which I would occasionally play Sinatra, Hammond organ star Jimmy Smith or Jack Jones LPs donated by friends. After my Elvis teenage days, I rarely forked out for things like records; my money went primarily on tarting myself up. Or, as time went on, trips abroad. As for the rest of the flat, you wouldn't care to examine your mattress too closely for very obvious signs of previous amorous engagements. Nor would the poky bathroom and loo withstand too much careful scrutiny. All this for £4 a week each.

Any effort to clean the place only happened if a dinner party was in view (menu: Birds Eye crispy cod fries, Birds Eye frozen chips (or watery tinned potatoes) and Birds Eye frozen peas. Frozen food, the 1950s forerunner of convenience food, became pre-eminent in the '60s, when supermarket shopping started to spring up – especially Birds Eye foods, the only brand to advertise their wares. This version of cookery was, to us, real effort. Our usual evening meal consisted of boiling up a packet of Knorr chicken soup – the precursor to Cup-a-Soup which arrived in 1972. Or munching on packets of Golden Wonder cheese & onion crisps, a novelty snack launched in 1962 that soon became a national obsession. If men were being entertained with our Birds Eye repertoire, someone (never me) might dig out the landlord's useless carpet sweeper and pointlessly introduce it to the floor. Or, if they were desperately keen to make a good impression, they might buy a box of the ultimate in post-prandial sophistication: After Eight thin mints, advertised then as something that snooty, fur-clad women kept in their Ferrari.

An only child, no matter where he or she lives, is a custodian of their own universe, their own solitary state. Being under the same roof as three other young women was a real struggle for me emotionally. I didn't row or have big arguments with them. I just felt... permanently uncomfortable with so many people around. I'd got the freedom I'd craved. But to an extent, I'd lost my privacy. Sharing a bedroom offered scant opportunity for love-ins.

All the others were from provincial homes: Denise and Sandra, sharing the downstairs bedroom, were from Leicester and Hampshire respectively. Denise was quiet, studying hard to be a teacher, pleasant but nondescript. She went home most weekends, which suited Sandra just fine because this allowed her to fully indulge in her two main proclivities. Let's be nice and call them her hobbies. The first was eating. Her family had some sort of farming connection on the south coast and she'd often drive to Waterloo station on Friday evening (she had her own little Mini, though none of us were ever invited into it) to meet the train and collect a big food hamper with goodies, including whole roast chickens, which her family had provided. Then she'd take the hamper back to her room, lock the bedroom door and chomp her way through it, only emerging over the weekend to go to the loo.

The other hobby also involved taking something into her room, locking the door and not emerging for 24 hours. Or more. But here Sandra wasn't quite as fortunate as she was with her weekly food parcels from home. Ideally, she'd substitute the hamper for a horny, living, breathing bloke. Nirvana for Sandra was to be holed up in the bedroom with both, but to the best of my knowledge, she never managed to pull this off. While clever and comfortably off with a good job as a legal secretary, Sandra definitely did not have it in the looks department. Plumpish, she was untidy, with unkempt hair and seriously badly dressed. Yet with rat-like cunning and guile, she could still manage to lure the odd unsuspecting male into her *Misery*-type boudoir and promptly lock the door. I don't know if she tied them to the bed or drugged them, the dreadful things that Kathy Bates did to poor old James Caan. But I did once see one victim emerge, shagged to his outer limits, after a weekend in randy Sandy's clutches. He looked like a man who'd just emerged from the rubble after an earthquake or a bomb – blinking, hardly believing his luck at still being alive. Free love, as much as a man could stand, had definitely arrived in the Finchley Road. But for some men it came at a higher price than they'd ever imagined. Sandy was relentless. I suppose she figured she'd better make the most of it since there was a chance it might never happen again.

Then there was my room-mate, at the opposite end of the spectrum from Sandy – and me too. At 19, Angela had arrived in London from a posh suburb of Manchester with big goals and big dreams. She wanted much, this girl. Her dad was a successful northern businessman and she'd grown up with riding lessons in Cheshire and private schooling, a far cry from my rackety East End childhood and abruptly terminated education. While Sandra wanted stuffed chickens and sex, preferably together, Angela wanted much more: a wealthy, good-looking husband who would drape her in Dior and Chanel, fully indulge her whims and catapult her into the upper echelons of society. Today, she'd probably be hanging out for a hedge fund manager. Then, there was no precise professional standard: he just had to be rich. Inherited money would do. But with her canny northern background she preferred a fortune made in business.

Angela was catty, derisive of much around us, which appealed to my own somewhat cynical take on life, and very manipulative. Yet she was also great fun. Her sarcastic tongue often surpassed my own somewhat acid dialogue, so we laughed a lot. She was pretty, with a snub nose, freckles, huge hazel eyes and curly hair. Though she was quite tall, her biggest worry was her lower half. Chubby thighs. Big legs. Half of her was a slim '60s dolly bird. The other half was less than average, when you consider how short skirts were and how important a neat derriere and a slim pair of legs could be in the overall scheme of things. Yet what she lacked in physical attributes she made up for with a sharp brain. She was foxy, long before the phrase became commonly used.

Unlike me, who merely reacted to events as they unfolded and used my brain only when I had to, Angela had it all planned out. She knew exactly where she was heading. Think of Thackeray's Becky Sharp from *Vanity Fair* and you won't be far off. After less than a year in London working as a secretary and not terribly impressed with what she'd landed thus far in the love stakes – a reasonably well-off, attractive and very attentive boy from the 'burbs, training to be a solicitor and poised to be the proud possessor of a big five or six-bedroom house in Weybridge – Angela came up with a bright idea. Why didn't the two of us hunt for bigger, better prey in a much better setting? New York, she calculated, would offer the single girl supremely better chances of bagging a multi-millionaire.

Neither of us had been there, of course. In the

popular imagination, it was the New York of myth and '60s movies like *The Apartment* or *Barefoot in the Park*, all honking yellow taxis, towering buildings, cocktail hours and fast-living, megabucks spenders. London had now emerged as a happening place, ever since the famous *Time* cover in 1966, proclaiming LONDON: THE SWINGING CITY. Yet the city was still dotted with wartime debris and shabby buildings – a long way from the fast-paced, slick consumer world, with all its 24/7 temptations, that Manhattanites were already accustomed to.

Today, we revisit the New York of that time through the carefully recreated prism of *Mad Men*, the advertising drama on TV. Ad agency secretaries in skyscraper buildings being shoehorned into a life of sizzle and consumer luxury by the likes of leading man Don Draper. Martinis at dawn. Even in the '60s, the idea of New York as a glamorous backdrop to a successful life was a global media-led phenomenon. It wasn't just the movies that sold New York as the epicentre of – well, everything glam. The books did too. An avid paperback reader, I'd already devoured *The Best of Everything*, the phenomenally successful 1950s Rona Jaffe book about Manhattan girls in acting or glamorous publishing jobs and single mums rescued by love or chased by married men on the make, four decades before *Sex and the City* made its mark. *Best…* impressed me: a high-octane story of young women choosing career and illicit affairs over the security of marriage. But I was even more impressed by what I was now reading in the pages of *Cosmopolitan*: the idea that you could pick and choose your men – and the way you ran your life.

The New York of my room-mate's dreams was very much a heady panorama of skyscraper luxury with rich Don Draper types seeking love in the arms of an English secretary. Perhaps not one with thunder thighs, but she'd find a way round that. As I've said, Angela wasn't going to let anything get in her way. And so somehow, in one of our many midnight conversations as we lay in our little single beds, talking boys, laughing at our flatmates' peccadilloes and sharing confidences, she convinced her restless, though distinctly unambitious room-mate with a love life that didn't bear too much close examination, to join her in a big enterprise. We'd be secretaries still. But in New York.

I must have said yes to the idea in one of my more reflective periods when I could see quite clearly that the Jeff thing, while exciting beyond belief, was even more emotionally hazardous than the previous road I'd embarked on with Bryan, who had been more or less fixed in his life, his ad-man world, his posh pad and his need for weed and booze. With Jeff, however, I didn't have a clue what he was up to. For all I knew, he could have been living part-time in another city. With another woman.

As for the New York idea, this was how it panned out.

At the time, English secretaries were very hot with New York bosses. The Brit accent, mostly, over the phone was a sure fire way to impress their peers or clients. Angela had spotted an ad for a London-based employment agency that specialised in helping secretaries with good experience relocate to New York. The agency would arrange it all, including the visa to work in the land of the free. Essentially, the deal was that you had to sign a contract to work exclusively for a New York secretarial agency as a temp. As Brits, our technical skills were deemed to be vastly superior to those of the locals from Queens, Brooklyn or Yonkers, who were, to be fair, probably used to a more diligent work ethic. What these agencies blithely ignored was how slack many London employers were in the '60s. By then, I'd job-hopped quite a bit. Secretaries were too often underemployed, little more than a status symbol.

The London agency, once they'd interviewed us and checked us out, took over all the paperwork. The Americans also insisted on a medical and various other administrative checks. The entire process, we were warned, would take several months. But what troubled me about it all was the somewhat draconian (to me) deal with the New York employment agency: they'd provide you with each placement as a temp. Once you'd done your two or three weeks at one place, they'd send you to another, and so on. But the contract you signed with them was binding. If you didn't like the work or jumped ship, you were out. Back to Blighty you must go. The agency would point you in the right direction to find suitable accommodation initially but you were more or less on your own when it came to finding a permanent place to live. The money, though, was good, much better than our London secretary's wages of £12–13 a week. Not quite double but close. Having Ange there would make the difference. It all pointed to a much better life, brighter prospects of finding more exciting men. Or so she convinced me at the time.

'You're not getting anywhere here, are you? Jeff'll ditch you one day and then where will you be?' she'd say in her somewhat blunt northern way. 'You don't wanna wind up with someone like that big fat fool, do you?' Meaning Bryan, which was cruel. But apt. She was spot on. None of my other girlfriends dared to push my nose into the reality of my dodgy affair with an obvious lothario. And eventually I'd confided in her about the illegal abortion and the Jeff/Bryan deception, so she knew exactly where I was coming from. What she said seemed to make sense, so I agreed.

Yet I had a niggling feeling that the agency dictating where I worked might not be such a good idea for someone like me, who resented any form of authority. I'd been exploiting my situation at the shoe company, had won a bit of autonomy and was lucky to have a boss who was hardly ever there. That worked for me. Job-wise, I could only hang around if I got a bit of freedom. I couldn't cope with a typing pool, for instance. A room full of girls at typewriters with a supervisor keeping an eagle eye on everything was far too authoritarian and disciplined. Less opportunity to – well, play it your own way.

Another big unconsidered weakness in The Plan was my relative lack of travel experience. Two teenage trips to Italy and one £30 all-in package holiday to Benidorm just before moving from Hackney do not a seasoned traveller make. And as with millions of ordinary people who now found sunshine packages affordable – thanks to tour companies like Clarksons or Horizon Holidays – my Benidorm trip had shown me there were certain drawbacks to these cheap sunshine deals. By the mid-1960s, the 400-page glossy Clarksons' holiday brochure was being pored over at night by families all over the country through the dark winter months, the shiny, enticing pictures of sun-baked sandy beaches and brand new, high-rise hotels in Spain proving irresistibly alluring to sun-starved, pale-skinned Brits.

In 1966, the year of my first-ever Spanish package, the average earnings were about £1,200 a year for men and around £600 a year for women. Which meant that the £30–£40 price tag had become affordable, something to save up for. Yet what the British holidaymaker didn't know – and how could they? – was that tour companies had spotted the huge potential of the cheap charter flight even in the 1950s. By the '60s they'd really got stuck in, doing deal after deal with eager Spanish hoteliers or developers, all desperate to cash in on the demand to accommodate the sun-starved millions from northern Europe. Alas, the demand for these holidays didn't match the ability of the Spaniards to fulfil their side of the contract, i.e. build the new hotels in time for the arrival of the tourist hordes.

Back then Spain was a very different place, still under the thumb of the dictator Franco, who had ruled with an iron fist since the 1930s. The hunger of Spanish businessmen and hoteliers to start making good money from the new tourism could not match the reality: this was the land of *mañana*. They just couldn't build the hotels fast enough. You'd book from the picture in the brochure, a beautiful brand new building, complete with swimming pool and palm-fringed, sunny terraces and pay for the holiday, only to discover at the eleventh hour that the builders were still very much on site. Or on extended siesta. If, indeed, they'd started working on the hotel at all.

I'd had this experience on my first Spanish trip with my friend Shirley. We'd arrived at Alicante airport to be met by the rep. 'Er… the hotel you booked isn't ready.' Shrug. 'We can put you up somewhere else. But it won't be what you booked. So sorry.' No hotel? What did they think we were there for? Today, with all those outraged holidaymakers going crazy, there'd be an irate and very public Twitter storm, with MDs making hurried statements at frenetic press conferences out on the steps of their headquarters, surrounded by nervous advisers. Yet then, with the package tourism industry still in its early stages, people understood less about their rights, their entitlements, so they tended to stay meek and go where they were told. Unless, like me, they were of the instantly militant type. I ranted. I shouted. I whipped up a storm of fury, helped by a few of the accompanying group of package tourists.

It worked. Within an hour Shirley and I were hustled onto a coach taking us to one of Benidorm's finest hotels, the Gran Hotel Delfin, on the edge of the amazing Poniente beach. To us, it was terribly luxurious. It proved to be a fairly uneventful fortnight, just loafing around the hotel pool in our bikinis with uncomfortably wired tops, wandering around the palm-fringed terraces, and venturing into hot, dusty Alicante for a few hours on a coach trip. Yet the dry, barren expanse around us, the huge tracts of undeveloped land and the sheer sense of the long history of this vast landscape where the sun burned down relentlessly, was the beginning of my decade-long love affair with Spain and its scented islands.

That was all I'd known of travel. Compare that to the idea of crossing the Atlantic to work and find a home, essentially alone in the Manhattan jungle. I'd blithely overlooked some hugely important things that I needed to consider, my homework if you like.

Jeff, of course, was constantly dismissive of my plan.

For a start, he didn't like the Yanks, as they were called. Amazingly, given their huge presence in London in wartime and the impact they'd made on many women's lives back then (the GI bride was a post-war phenomenon that lingered on in British minds for decades), he was like so many of his generation. These were the guys who were too young for war but had had to do two years of national service in the 1950s and still harboured disdain for Americans. Or, come to that, his rejection of the idea of most people who didn't come from our sceptred isle. 'They think they won the war' was his view on all Americans, 'but they bloody didn't.' And so on. Or I'd get: 'You're a Londoner, what do you need to go there for?' 'And you're my bird, anyway. You don't really wanna go.' And so on.

Yet when the moment came for my big medical at the American Embassy, I turned up and had the obligatory examination and chest x-ray. I was going, and sod Jeff. Even so, I told no one else about the plan, apart from the other girls in the flat. But that was it – not my parents or girlfriends. Even my best friend, Lolly, now a mum of two and still living in east London, knew nothing of it.

And then that letter arrived. At last. What it told me was this: I'd cleared the medical and been given the visa. Inside was the paperwork to authorise my application to work in New York. Angela's application too was being processed, though her medical had been booked for a couple of weeks after mine. Soon she too trotted off to

Grosvenor Square. This was it. Soon we'd be sipping cocktails in a skyscraper, typing letters and making eyes in the elevator at the handsome execs with the sexy Yank drawl – in short, the envy of our flatmates left behind in the big, tacky flat on the Finchley Road. Yet destiny had other ideas. One afternoon at work, I got a call from Angela. She was sobbing her heart out.

'They won't accept me because the x-ray shows I've got TB,' she told me. 'I can't go. I'm going home tomorrow: my mother's coming down to collect me.' Instead of flying to Don Draper's arms and a life of highballs, Angela was destined to return up north, take her medication and recover in the comfort of her big family home. It wasn't a very severe case of TB; indeed she was lucky to discover it because she insisted she had no symptoms. But the US authorities were no longer interested in her application. Our plan was wrecked. Unless, of course, I was prepared to go it alone. Yes or no?

I never regarded myself as a shoulda/woulda/coulda type person. So many of us go through life saying, 'If that had happened, if I'd done that, well, maybe...' Yet there was never a single occasion, even when things were quite bleak later on, when I looked back and questioned the decision I'd made not to fly solo and be a secretary in Manhattan.

I toyed with the idea, a fairly bold move for the times, even for someone like me. But while I acted daring, I secretly remained as unsure of myself as most young women were then. I had told no one. I tried hard to envisage myself, without any familiar faces, in a strange place a long way away from London, and it wasn't long before I had to admit to myself that I just wasn't up for it. It was all too daunting. And, anyway, I didn't feel bad about not going. After all, it hadn't been my idea. Perhaps if I'd been totally disillusioned with London life, it might have propelled me forward. Yet I still doubt it.

New York – and the USA itself – fascinated Brits back in the '60s because it seemed to be a Technicolor world we largely knew nothing of, filled with huge fridges, air con, big cars, cocktails and full-on consumer luxury. OK, we were on the way to consumerism then, ever since the mini-explosion of advertising for clothes, cars and gadgets, Sunday supplement style, had started to exert its influence on us. American culture was worshipped and exalted way beyond ours by many in the UK, yet I didn't see a need to acknowledge or experience this by gracing the place with my presence.

A true Londoner since childhood, when I'd first climbed all those stairs up to the Monument in the City and stared down at London from above, I'd known that despite the grime, the dirt, the shabby, lingering after-effect of war, here was one of the world's greatest cities. My city, with all its history, its buildings, its pageantry, its traditions. And now, thanks to our chums across the pond and the defining moment of the *Time* article of 1966 – a superlative PR exercise the effect of which lingered for decades – I'd fully absorbed all the London hype. The real action was here, on London's streets, in the tiny clubs and boutiques that were popping up all over the place. And in bed with Jeff.

I knew a girl who did head for Manhattan in the '60s to type and find a better life. She too came from London's East End, was an only child like me and hankered for a brighter perspective. And she got it. She's still there, married to a genial local, living happily in the 'burbs, sunning herself at their second home in Florida in winter. She'd had a few tricky moments, initially living in a women-only hostel in Manhattan where male visitors were forbidden. But she'd stuck with it – because she believed in her dream, knew it was right for her.

I was far too immature and undisciplined to embark on that adventure in such a determined way. You need passion, a drive for reinvention and a fierce desire for change. Had I not liked my first or second temp assignment, I'd have promptly walked out – and probably had to fly back home in a hurry. What the whole thing represented to me, as thought up by the persuasive Angela, was the idea of an adventure, another lark. But the determination to alter my life completely, create another mode of living just wasn't there. I was an unfocussed, sensation-seeking girl without real ambition. I'd grown up with parents who more or less lived for the moment, so to me that was life. Today was what mattered. Which set me on a hedonistic, pleasure-seeking path for a long, long time.

As for Angela, it all happened for her anyway. Once she'd recovered, she came back to London and found a new job with a big American multinational company. There, one sweet day, a good-looking young executive walked over to her desk and started chatting her up. He was from a wealthy English family based in America. Did she fancy going out to dinner? It didn't all happen overnight, mind you. He was a catch, but no pushover. She had to plot to keep him interested. One ploy involved getting her flatmates to send her a huge bouquet of flowers, no signature, to the office one day, much, as she'd hoped, to his chagrin.

In the end, it all worked out as she'd wished and they wed. Many years later, I ran into her by chance outside Harrods in Knightsbridge. I won't say she was dripping with diamonds but she looked... well, just incredibly rich. They had a flat in Sloane Square, she told me. There was a second home, a big house near the lake in Geneva. You can only stand back and admire the woman who knows, right from day one, exactly what she wants.

CHAPTER FOUR

THE GO-GO GIRL FROM GUILDFORD

A small, steamy Italian café just off Oxford Circus, in the early spring of 1968. The smell of fried eggs lingers in the air. A girl in a smart, black Wallis double-breasted wool coat with a fake fur collar is seated at a Formica table, furiously scanning the small ads in the *Evening Standard*.

I am desperate to move. With the collapse of the New York plans and Angela's dramatic move back north, I want to make a getaway. Now. The atmosphere in the flat has changed a lot. Angela's replacement, Shoshana, an Israeli student, moved in six months ago. She has hordes of friends from home, some in London to study – but also wanting to party like crazy in the swinging city. Sandy and Denise welcome the diversion of having these boisterous, lively friends of Shoshana around. Sandy even manages to beguile one of the boys, Sam, into her boudoir oubliette (unlike the unfit Brits, Sam, who has recently served in the Israeli army, emerges the next day without any visible signs of exertion). Meeting the young Israelis is a learning curve for me. In conversation, they're blunt, direct. What you see is what you get. A couple of the men are quite good-looking. Yet they're so direct in their ways, without any subtlety of manner, I find it difficult to relate to them. English men are like this too, sometimes, but a lot of them manage to hide it. With the Israeli men, it's all a bit 'Me Tarzan, you Jane'.

To an only child, already struggling with a sharing situation and craving a degree of solitude, the arrival of a new group of people is a disruption too far. Shoshana's pals pile into the flat *en masse*, stroll into the kitchen, open cupboards and drawers, hunt for food and cutlery. Whatever they do find, usually thoughtfully provided by Shoshana, they cheerfully eat, plonking themselves down in the living room, plates on laps, laughing and joking in Hebrew. I query all this, of course. How come they just walk in and do what they like?

'This is how we live in Israel,' they explain. 'We share everything. If you come to our home, we don't mind you sharing our food.'

I have a Jewish background, but this is my first glimpse of people from the homeland. The six-day Arab-Israeli war of June 1967 was a landmark victory for the state of Israel, just 20 years old. But the ideas, the pioneering socialist principles behind the building of the new country, which meant many people working on the land together, sharing all their resources, go right over my head, sadly. I don't enjoy or understand how rewarding it can be to be part of a group. I like Shoshana. She's a lively person. But I shrink back from the group's noisy company: I just want my own space. Essentially, I want to share a flat with one person, someone more like me.

I'd never quite related to Sandra and Denise. They were too drab, for a start. Angela was focused and ambitious, alien to me, yet there were shared obsessions: men, fashionable clothes and eye makeup – her false lashes had to be seen to be believed, perfectly working the big, doe-eyed '60s Biba look (used to powerful effect by model-turned-photographer Sarah Moon). She had also been consistently honest in her opinions – believing, with some justification, that my torrid affair with Jeff was leading to Nowheresville – but the other two, while they never said anything to my face, clearly turned their noses up at my plebian lover. Respectable girls from safe backgrounds, they didn't care to respond to his Jack the lad joshing and innuendo.

Sandy of the locked boudoir was as rampant in her habits as any swinger of the time (when she could rope them in), yet in conversation you'd have thought she was Mother Teresa. I'd get sneers and funny looks from her if she 'tidied' the lounge and picked up my discarded copies of *Nova*, the ultimate hip, glossy style magazine with a revolutionary visual flair and a no-holds-barred approach to hitherto hidden topics like abortion, drugs, homosexuality, VD and wife-swapping. ALL MEN ARE BASTARDS was one cynical headline in bold letters above an article about men and their naughty ways. I laughed, promptly cut it out and stuck it over my bed. Sandy didn't see the funny side. '*Is this yours?*' she would say with disdain, holding an offending copy of the magazine between two fingers as if *Nova*'s mere presence in the flat was enough to transform us all into sex-crazed nymphos, charging starkers down the Finchley Road in pursuit of any male.

Nova, launched in 1965 (and killed off, ultimately, by the arrival of *Cosmo* in the early 1970s), really was the magazine for its time. But not every woman was quite ready to openly display her enthusiasm for the onset of the sexual revolution. My flatmate's expectations for living in the big smoke were, essentially, a mirror image of the aspirations of the girls I'd gone to school with: the ring, the big white floaty meringue, the semi in the quiet neat streets of identical semis in Wembley, Gants Hill or Surbiton. And maternity smocks. As soon as possible, please.

By now, my parents, Molly and Ginger, had adjusted to the idea of me, their already worryingly wayward 20-something daughter, sharing a flat, though my relationship with my dad remained very much at arm's length. I'd visit them every couple of weeks, less if I could get away with it. I still detested the poky flat off Shacklewell Lane where I'd grown up. Even visiting it briefly disturbed me: the dirty stone stairs, the noisy timber yard opposite, the flies buzzing round the rubbish chute in summer. Sometimes I could time my visit to avoid Ginger. Saturday afternoon in the football season was ideal because mostly he was off enjoying a home game of his beloved Spurs. Then, Molly would make me a favourite lunch – tinned sardines on toast to start, roast chicken with all the trimmings to follow and I'd sit there stuffing my face, after filling her in on some of my news. I gossiped about friends of mine that she knew, though I never mentioned my love life – and she didn't ask. Or we'd arrange to meet up in Oxford Street and do a tour of the shops and have a bite to eat in a Corner House– a girly pastime that continued for years.

Molly was working now, two days a week, selling underwear in Jax on the corner of Dalston Lane with Saturdays off. Working wives existed back then, of course. But those that did work tended to do it out of real necessity or need. Men still furiously resisted any idea of their wives' independence – and Ginger was light years away from being what we now call a 'new man'. Yet both my parents had, somehow, adjusted to their recently changed circumstances, with Molly working to keep them afloat now that my dad had lost his bookie business.

'Your dad's got a job,' she told me cheerfully on one of

my visits home several months after I'd left. 'He's working as a clerk in the accounts department at the British Medical Association in Tavistock Square. The money's not good but they've said it will go up.'

'Maybe he'll be a thousand-a-year man, after all, Mum,' I quipped sarcastically. The phrase, 'a thousand-a-year man' was bandied about at the time frequently as a marker of mid-1960s prosperity. To me, such a statement in relation to my dad, Ginger, was a huge joke. A thousand a year – £20 a week – was merely a few big rounds of drinks for his punters when he was flinging his cash around the pub in his long lost days in the early years of the decade as the last of the big-spending bookies.

'Well, at least it's going to be easier for us now, Jac,' Molly said, her loyalty to her man undiminished by time or circumstance. Instead of being bitter and twisted about the fact that she had been forced to go out to work in her late forties and was still stuck in a post-war Dalston grot hole, Molly held fast to the positives. OK, so they'd had the good times, lived it up while others had it lean. Now times were improving for others and they'd hit a rough patch, yet she was determined not to look back with rancour. Or give my dad a hard time about his weaknesses or mistakes. Other women might have been angry or mean-spirited about their situation, but not my mum. Anyway, working as an underwear sales lady meant a decent staff discount, a third off the asking price of anything in the shop. So her new Triumph Feel Free bra, priced at 29/11 (30 bob), had cost her just £1, she informed me. I too could benefit from this generous discount if I wished.

'I'll get one for you, Jac, for next time you come,' chirped Molly, happy to be doing something – anything – for me beyond the occasional meal. I knew, deep down, how much she missed having me around, looked forward to our brief outings or my visits. Her smiley face whenever I turned up told me the real story. Yet there was never a word of protest or recrimination that I'd fled the nest.

Nonetheless, this news about Dad's work was quite startling: other than his bookie life, my dad had never actually held down a proper job. Even before they'd married he'd led a peripatetic existence, travelling around, 'on the knocker' – selling household goods door to door. Now here he was, a 50-something with a regular 9-5 wage. And a pension. Respectability at last. Paid holidays too. They'd already booked a week's holiday on the coast, in the Albion Hotel at Broadstairs, something they'd never done when racing timetables dominated my dad's life and he was unable to get a whole week off to take the missus on holiday.

'D' you think he'll stick it, Mum?' I pondered, pushing back the empty plate, feeling uncomfortably full after the first decent meal I'd had for ages beyond the shop-bought cheese rolls, occasional tubs of Eden Vale cottage cheese and the Knorr packet soups I consumed most of the time.

'Oh yes. They love him in the office. They think he's really funny.'

That was Ginger. A non-stop bar-room clown. A stream of jokes for every occasion.

I was somewhat taken aback that this posh-sounding doctor's professional body would take to his Cockney banter and repartee but opposites attract, eh? What I was way too immature to understand was that Ginger's confidence, seriously dented by the collapse of his business, must have received a huge boost by the offer of a steady job – let alone having his new colleagues laughing themselves silly at his wisecracks.

I mulled over all this as I scanned the *Standard*, my eyes peeled for any ad that showed potential, musing over my dad's somewhat lucky break which had been engineered by Molly – she spotted the BMA job ad in the same newspaper. It's good news, of course it is. But I still can't shake off my disgust at how he'd blown all their cash, nose-dived the business into failure, left them almost penniless – and how he'd blighted my early years with his drinking and possessive behaviour. Out of the hated environment I was and out I'd stay. All I needed now was a new person to share a flat with… And there it was, a line in black type, nestling in between all the other ads. 'Girl wanted to share flat in central London,' followed by a phone number.

Enter Rosemary. She didn't actually have a flat to share, she'd been living abroad, in Turkey, she told me over the phone. She'd worked in a club in Istanbul as a go-go dancer. Now she wanted to find someone suitable to share with first and then we could look together for a good place. Should we meet up? I was intrigued, impressed. This definitely wasn't another prim, hypocritical provincial girl. Here was someone sophisticated who'd already got out there and tasted life and experience. This girl was way ahead of me in the travel stakes. I'd only sampled that one package holiday to Benidorm. Nothing like as exotic or exciting as dancing in a cage in a Turkish nightclub…

If I was a very competitive sort of girl, I might have been put off by Rosemary's appearance. She looked exactly how every fashion-hungry young girl in London wanted to look – the archetypal dolly bird of the era, a real head-turner. Shoulder-length, straight fair hair, a tall, skinny frame with small boobs, long lean limbs, the shortest of skirts and an appropriate air of disdain. A true babe, just three years older than me.

I heard her story in another Italian café over a watery minestrone and a stale roll. Her family came from Guildford, Surrey. She'd been in Turkey for two years because she was engaged to a Turkish boy who'd only recently gone into the army to do the Turkish equivalent of National Service. While living in Istanbul, he with his family, she in a tiny apartment, she'd worked at night as a go-go dancer. Istanbul in the mid-1960s was at the very edge of what was known then as the hippie trail to India. So it attracted large numbers of young travellers from Europe, the US and elsewhere, mostly dropouts or Vietnam draft-dodgers en route to India and Kathmandu, Nepal, in search of the wisdom of the east and enlightenment (and dope).

Skimpily clad, dancing on the podium in a smoky, crowded club night after night before a throng of mainly northern European expats, waving those long, lean limbs – complete with long, skinny boots – was one way of earning enough money to live there and be with the Turkish boy. But he'd be stuck in the army for at least another two years so it made sense to come back home, work hard and save up for their future. She couldn't live with her family in Surrey because she wanted to live near the West End, close to work. She'd already settled into a good job, as a manager for an employment agency. These were truly boom years for agencies like Brook Street Bureau, Conduit, Alfred Marks and Drake Personnel: commissions for those helping to recruit the unending stream of office workers needed in central London were good. A manager could earn a basic £800 a year – a bit less than a secretary in the area – but they could double their earnings in commissions for placing staff. So she could save like crazy.

'Mehmet writes all the time and he goes insane if I

even mention another guy so I'm not interested in anyone else,' she told me (it proved to be the pure bullshit line she spun to all). 'And sometimes he sends his friends over to keep an eye on me, so they might turn up any time,' she warned. 'Turkish men are incredibly jealous.'

I shrugged. The odd Turk at the gate didn't sound like a problem (little did I know). Then I briefly told her about the now-you-see-him, now-you-don't Jeff experience, explaining that I did my own thing when he wasn't around. 'I'm on the pill,' I informed her. 'I want to do whatever I like.' At this news, my potential flatmate's expression changed. Initially quite smiley and relaxed, she now looked distinctly nervous, unsettled by this clear admission that someone was happily at it whenever they fancied someone.

'Ooh, I couldn't do anything like that,' she said, not quite looking me in the eye. 'I'm engaged, anyway.'

Rosie's long-distance romance wasn't that unusual. Foreign boyfriends or fiancés were becoming quite common by then. Our mums and aunts might have tripped the light fantastic on the dance floor – or done a bit more afterwards – with gum-chewing GIs in wartime. Or they smooched uniformed men from other countries at a local hop. But cheap foreign travel for my generation in the '60s had wrought changes: young, single British girls, much more free with their favours than their equivalents in Latin countries, were frequently hot bait for love-starved, passionate, ball-scratching Euro locals.

Holiday romances, oh, how they lit up the mundane, everyday lives of so many girls. Today you read about grandmothers on the rampage, hot-footing it to the Gambia for love or marriage with lean lads young enough to be their sons. Back then, it was much more straightforward: young, late teen or 20-something office girl gets two-week sun tan by day and a surfeit of passionate promises of eternal love in very broken *Engleesh* by night. Accompanied by the delicate dropping of bikini bottoms on the sand. (Knickers on tiled hotel room floors were still uncommon, since beady-eyed hoteliers were not yet up for guests dragging their newest squeeze back to the package-deal hotel). Hot, sticky love in another climate. No contest against life back home when you consider the reality then of the other 50 weeks of the year: a shabby office or factory with strip lighting and a monotonous routine, permanently grey skies, a packed, smoke-filled local pub – and a steady, stolid boyfriend more preoccupied with football scores or closing time than wooing his woman.

One work friend, Annie, had a package holiday in Gibraltar and a fleeting, passionate affair with a local, married, tour guide. Only to discover, in a south London doctor's surgery several months later, that she'd remember that holiday for ever. (Annie was a large, if healthy lady, and her symptom-free pregnancy went totally undetected for seven months. It sounds bizarre but that's exactly what happened.) Another girlfriend,

Jeanette, flew out to a Spanish resort at every opportunity to be with Miguel, a holiday rep for Clarksons Tours. It fizzled out. Pat, a tall blonde from Kent I'd worked with previously in Soho, had a hopeless and somewhat frustrating relationship with another Miguel, a waiter in Loret de Mar. She spent her free time at home learning Spanish. He used his free time for other tall blondes, some also called Pat. My school friend Lolly was married to Michael, an Italian waiter at the Savoy, and had a family of two. Another girl from Dalston, Georgina, had met Paolo, a dark-eyed southern Italian, in a Soho disco and they wound up married. And so on.

Boyfriend or not, Rosemary would be a good person to share with, I figured. She talked conventionally but she didn't really look it. Always wildly impressed by the glossy, fashionable look (my mum's lifelong obsession with dressing up and looking good probably had much to do with this), I did have a bad case of hair envy. Rosemary's hair was naturally straight and silky. Mine wasn't. I'd resorted to positioning a hefty, straight blonde hairpiece over my frizzy, dyed-blonde mop (with dark roots) to get the right dolly-bird look. Bad hair or not, a decision was made. We'd find a flat and split the rent.

Rosemary came up with something first. It sounded great but alas, I didn't have the cash. It was a flat in a posh red brick block in Abbey Road, St Johns Wood, just across the street from the studios and the zebra crossing the Beatles would march across into rock history with

Abbey Road in 1969. In those days, long before flat rentals were regulated, London landlords would advertise flats quoting not just a rent but a chunk of money, sometimes called key money, which was effectively a deposit. Key money is no longer legal. But then, there was nothing to stop landlords asking for it. Or people coughing up. Sometimes the landlord's ad would quote an annual rent to be paid in one go, say £250, including furniture and fittings (usually pretty disgusting old stuff they couldn't be bothered to chuck out).

The swanky flat in the red brick block was £15 a week but the landlord wanted a down payment of £600 cash for a three-year lease. But my £300 share would be far too much for me, a woman with a wardrobe stocked with crepe dresses from Radley but who couldn't afford the real deal, Ossie Clarke, the superman of '60s and '70s designers. (Rosemary had the cash – and a much better wardrobe with buttery soft leather jackets and even a fur coat.) But about a week later I struck gold in the *Standard*: the ideal location, just off the southern end of the Finchley Road in St John's Wood. No key money, only a month's rent in advance. £10 a week. One small bedroom.

Finding a habitable flat to share on a secretary's pay was extremely difficult. London's evening newspapers, the *Evening News* and the *Standard*, had several editions on the street through the day. All the flat-letting ads were in the *Standard* – but if you bought it late in the day, sorry, too late. The few affordable flats advertised were always gone. Or the phone number was permanently engaged (off the hook, usually, when a pissed-off landlord would tire of the endless stream of calls). If a landlord had stipulated a time to view, you'd turn up at the flat at 9 am to find a long queue of people outside the front door. Yet if you bought the paper the minute it came out in the morning and there was no set viewing time, you had a chance.

The flat was on the corner of Circus Road, above a baker's shop. It, too, was a short walk away from Abbey Road Studios and the famous zebra crossing, and minutes away the West End, work, shops, clubs, everything we needed. There was even a deli opposite, Panzers, so there'd be no problem with having to cook or food shopping. There were pubs at either end of Circus Road. Regent's Park was just a walk away. It really was the ideal launch pad for two 20-somethings, right in the heart of it all. There was one slight drawback: it was even shabbier – and much smaller — than the Finchley Road flat. Up the stairs, ancient loo and bathroom on the landing, then at the top, the square, sparse kitchen directly facing what had been just one room, now divided by a landlord's paper-thin partition wall, into a very small living area (just one battered old sofa and two chairs) and an even smaller bedroom. The bedroom, overlooking the street, was just big enough for two single beds and an ancient wardrobe.

Space really was at a premium. Both rooms were decorated with a poster of Chairman Mao, left there by the previous tenant. There was a phone on the living room floor, a luxury after the coin box of the last place. And, because it was above a bakery, mice scooting across the kitchen floor eventually became as regular a feature of our lives as the eager young men who'd drop in on us virtually all the time, en route to and from the centre of town. Talk about location, location, location. This place wasn't just convenient, it was a bloke magnet.

There was no TV – hardly a source for concern since we were rarely at home long enough to sit down and watch it. But I had acquired a valuable asset via my old job at the electronics company – an early-model answering machine. I'd been surreptitiously given it as a parting gift on my last day there. It took me months to find someone to set it up for us, but eventually we had the answer to the age-old problem of Waiting For Him to Phone: a machine (essentially a tape recorder connected to the phone line) that played a message recorded in my breathiest tones glibly informing all callers that Jacky and Rosie were out – but they'd love to hear from you, so please leave your name and number…

So new were these machines that many people couldn't cope with them. There were more sounds of people hanging up than messages left. Or there were sarcastic jokers who'd say, 'The one thing I don't wanna do is speak to Jacky or Rosie.' Some comedians would sing – but not reveal their identity. It was definitely progress in knowing if the men you wanted to ring were calling. But not much. People couldn't go out and buy these things cheaply the way they do now. BT would only permit them to be rented. Signing up to rent one – on a five-year contract – was a hefty financial commitment. It was a big day in the office at the electronics company when John Cleese, already a BBC name with *The Frost Report* and on the cusp of his success with *Monty Python*, rang up to order two, one for home, one for office. Yet they remained a novelty, really. After all, 60 per cent of households in the country didn't even have a phone.

Jeff didn't take to Rosemary. This was odd, as she looked every inch the desirable hot babe. 'I don't like her,' he said thoughtfully, after the first meeting. 'There's something funny, like she's got something to hide.' Jeff's instincts were finely tuned. There was a secret back story to Rosemary. But neither of their hidden worlds would be revealed to me just yet. When I did start to learn a bit more about my new flatmate, it was nothing more than a partial glimpse of her world, that summer of '68, when things started to change a little bit for me.

Until moving in with Rosemary, who created her own social scene around us, I'd still gone to clubs, sometimes with friends. I'd already abandoned the West End places like Tiffany's in Piccadilly (easy to pull there but the men were too dodgy) or the Whisky-A-Go-Go (ditto) for the more fashionable clubs further West, like the De Vere in Kensington and, on the odd occasion, the musicians' hang out, places like the Cromwellian in Cromwell Road.

The De Vere was my favourite. One reason I liked it was that just getting the guy on the door to let you in was a challenge of sorts. It was free for girls, but only the nod from the fat, bald man behind the small table at the top of the stairs would get you in. It seemed you had to be the right kind of babe. The De Vere had two floors. On the first was a small, intimate kind of bar with banquettes and a few tables and chairs while the top floor had the dancing area. No live music: just the latest big hits such as 'Ride Your Pony' (Lee Dorsey), 'Keep on Running' (the Spencer Davies hit), 'Respect' (the Otis Redding song that Aretha Franklin made her own), 'The Letter' (The Box Tops) and The Foundations' 'Baby, Now That I've Found You'. The music, whether Motown or Stevie Winwood, would become legend, but unlike my go-go flatmate, I was never a very enthusiastic dancer. The cool way to do it was to make the appropriate hip-shaking gestures, copying the better dancers' moves, managing to keep in time – and looking as if you couldn't really be bothered.

I wasn't a great beauty, but I had smooth-skinned youth on my side. And I was quite slim, dressed to look even thinner, usually in a tight sheath dress, heels as high as I could manage, though I was never able to walk confidently in them. Perched on those four-inch heels, about as non-athletic as you could get, I was a wobbler, a totterer. Yet high heels are part of your essential armoury when you're permanently on the pull (that's why you see so many 50-something women and beyond hanging onto them). They elevate. They push out your best bits, to go with the teased hair, the lavish all-over spray of Diorama, my favourite of all the Dior fragrances, no longer around now.

I had my triumphs at the De Vere. At one point, I'd run into a fascinating blond out-of-work actor, Derek, with whom I spent a steamy 48 hours in his flat off Shepherds Market in Mayfair – and never saw again. Another time at the De Vere I acquired what is now called a fuck buddy, Nick, a dark-haired hunk of Greek origin, who lived with a model in a mansion block in Elgin Avenue, Maida Vale. Nick would often call on weekends to pick me up to join him in their flat – while she was away on modelling trips. Nice guy, eh? Nick was memorable for his tiny red TR4 sports car – and was incredibly well hung. He had a kind of saturnine, sardonic allure. I had a distinct penchant for moody, surly men – a hangover, maybe from the early days of my Elvis lust. The Nick thing went on for about a year or so, though I never had a clue what he did for a crust. But if they didn't tell you, who cared? I was in it for the excitement, the kicks, the moment itself. There was no goal, just a theme – girl meets different men, dives in, enjoys what she likes the look of, discards or ignores the rest. The men, of course, were just being opportunistic, simply because more women were now up for it. Everything you heard or read about new sexual freedoms seemed to conspire to give people more latitude.

But not everyone at the De Vere has a good time. One Thursday night, I am on the tiny dance floor, shrugging, moving carefully, ignoring my partner and contemplating an early night, when I spot a familiar figure on the edge of the dance floor. A tubby man, going to seed. Glaring at me. He's got a bloody cheek, I think to myself. He was the one that ran off. Bryan. It is, by now, well over 18 months since my Central line trip and Bryan has totally ignored my existence in that time. Of course I've been hurt by this, Bryan had, after all, been a pivotal person in my life, the first big affair. Yet the deception with the two men had been a messy situation I'd mostly succeeded in shaking off. Now I'm occasionally seeing Jeff, sleeping with anyone I like the look of, working out of my shoe company cubby hole, pretending to be a man with a double-barrelled name.

'Tart!' Bryan hisses at me as I leave the dance floor to go down to the ladies loo. 'You're a bloody *tart*!'

What's going on in his mind? I have no idea. Am I a tart because of what I'd done, used my wits to get out of what, for me, was an impossible, intolerable situation and now he's guessed that I lied? Or am I a tart because I'm out and about on the pull?

Now, as I make my way back up the stairs, he's standing there, blocking the entrance to the bar, glass of double scotch in hand, looking distinctly dishevelled. He's even more overweight, really slobby now. His clothes are creased. There are food stains on his expensive silk tie. This, I tell myself, is a frustrated man who can't get anyone into bed. That's why he's so angry. He had a regular bed partner. Once. She's out there now, on the pull and loving it. He can't find a replacement. Why? Because he's morphed into a saddo barfly. I don't bother to hide my opinions. 'You're only pissed off with me because no one wants to sleep with you,' I hiss. No sooner do the words fall from my lips than I see by his expression that I've hit home. Hard. That's my trouble. It's one thing to see the truth but not everyone wants to hear it. Yet again, I say the unsayable without a thought for what happens next. My brand new, sleeveless skimmer dress from Fenwicks, costing nearly £10, is quickly dripping double scotch and ice. A dry-cleaning bill of three shillings and sixpence awaits me. A furious Bryan, frustrated male incarnate, has chucked the contents of the glass at me.

'Bitch!' he yells. 'Fucking bitch!' He lurches down the stairs, still clutching the empty glass, down past the doorman, out into Ken High Street. And out of my life. For good.

CHAPTER FIVE

BANDAGE MAN

Rosemary isn't just older, more experienced and worldly than my previous flatmates. She is a man magnet. Flashily dressed, a woman that men tend to gawp at on the street, she creates a considerable flurry of attention around her. I stop using clubs to meet men: at that point, they seem to be swarming around us. All the time. Parties. Friends of friends, determinedly collecting phone numbers, ringing up out of the blue, even if I don't remember them. Men I'd run into at drinks after work.

Some just become friends. One long-lasting friendship comes about in a rather odd way, though the incident underlines my far-too-casual attitude towards going off into the night with total strangers. In a jam-packed hallway at a very noisy, crowded party in Swiss

Cottage, I get chatting to Laurie, a journalist turned public relations man from West Hampstead. Laurie is a few years older than me and we have something in common: a shared appreciation of French and Italian movies. It turns out we've both worked for the same foreign film distribution company, Gala Films, in Soho at different times in the early '60s. Soon, he's proffering a friendly toke from a joint of weed, which I refuse. 'I've just moved into this great place with my friend John,' he informs me, taking a huge drag of the joint and nearly choking with the effort. 'It's a big mansion flat. We've both got our own space, so it works really well.'

I don't fancy him one bit. So it is probably quite daft to accept his offer to drive me to West Hampstead to inspect his new premises about half an hour later. But I am an endlessly curious girl in many ways. I really do want to check the flat out, have a look round, see how others are living. And Laurie is Jewish, which to me is a sort of dating shorthand for safe, sober, highly unlikely to be a lunatic rapist. I'll have a good look round. Then I'll get him to run me home afterwards. But once inside his space, which is essentially a decent-sized bedroom masquerading as a studio, with armchairs and a sofa, things take a rapid turn for the worse. All conversation ceases. Laurie lies on his big double bed expectantly. I sit on an armchair. Now I've seen the flat – which is actually quite spacious, with stained glass panels in the front door and an impressively thick carpet on the stairs – I'm ready to depart. Er… could he run me home?

Silence. The PR man's eyes are now closed.

'Look, I wanna go home. If you don't wanna drive, you can call me a cab,' I offer.

More silence. Then a gentle snore. He's asleep. Or rather, I know immediately he's just pretending to be asleep. He'd got my phone number earlier at the party. He probably had hopes of some action, but I've dashed them by making it clear I want out. Sorry, Laurie, but you don't get off that lightly. Be a gent. Play the game. So I try again. Nicely. 'Can you call me a cab, please?' Nothing. Another fake snore (he's a crap actor).

Now I'm really angry. The fact that he is pretending to be asleep in order to get out of all this is so pathetic. OK, so I don't want to play ball. Does he have to be so bloody infantile about it all? Sod him! And without any thought whatsoever, I pick up the nearest object, a heavy Murano glass ashtray, and fling it with all my might across the room so it hits the opposite wall with a resounding thud. Whack! Hey, he's wide awake!

'What have you done?' he snarls, rushing over to inspect the damage – a big dent in his bedroom wall. 'I'll have to pay the bloody landlord for this!' Then he dives out, goes next door to his flatmate's quarters and returns, red faced, a few minutes later. 'There's a cab coming,' he tells me, ushering me out into the narrow hallway. 'Get out!'

I clomp down the stairs and sure enough, a black cab pulls up in a few minutes. I promptly go home and forget all about it...

But Laurie, a Scorpio with a mean streak, does not forget. A respectably reared boy from Golders Green, he is not used to such displays of girlie tantrum. He and John, his flatmate, hatch a cunning revenge plot, commando style. They know where I live because I've told him I'm above the baker on the corner of Circus Road, so the pair decide to teach the lairy girl a lesson. That Sunday, they climb into John's little MGB and drive to my flat. In the car, they have a big bucket of cold water, ready and waiting.

The idea is this. They'll ring the bell, I'll appear at the door and, whoosh, I'll get the bucket of cold water treatment, pure payback for denting his wall. Waterboarding, north-west London style. Neat trick, eh? I know none of this until a couple of months later, when Laurie rings the flat. 'I'm the guy whose wall you ruined with an ashtray,' he says. He tells me about the revenge plan which misfired, probably because the doorbell, typically, was faulty and often didn't work. They'd rung, the waiting bucket at their side. They'd stood there expectantly, waiting for the joyful moment of Laurie's revenge. But no one came down. Such is the way friendships are born: Laurie and I remained friends over the years.

Much later, when I asked him why he'd pretended to

be asleep, he explained it all to me. It was mostly down to the clothes I wore. 'Your tits were almost hanging out and you had a really short skirt on. To blokes like me, always on the hunt for nookie, that was a signal that you were definitely up for it. And once you said you'd come to my flat, I thought I was well in.'

Mixed messages, eh? There is, of course, a well-worn argument that if women dress provocatively, they shouldn't be surprised if men react accordingly – because men are men, after all. My argument is: I defined myself back then as a girl of my time, certainly, partly by the way I dressed. But I was also at a point where I was very conscious that I'd choose who I'd sleep with, not the other way round. Things had changed. Women no longer had to sit waiting patiently for men to summon them. If men got the wrong signals sometimes, it was just too bad…

At that point, the accelerating pace of life in Circus Road involved a bit of double-dating. Jeff suggested fixing Rosemary up with one of his friends, Eddie, another, even taller blond Michael Caine look-alike. Off we went in Eddie's new Ford Escort to the little Bistro d'Agran, tucked away behind Harrods in Knightsbridge, red-and-white check tablecloths, candles lighting up the tiny space, tough minute steaks that were difficult to chew, the ubiquitous Black Forest gateau afterwards. Rosemary took a distinct fancy to Eddie, an obvious charmer with a good line in salesman's patter, but alas,

Eddie was very married and vanished back to the outer 'burbs after our night out, never to be seen again, despite Rosemary's repeated enquiries after his existence.

On another occasion, Jeff insisted on introducing Rosemary to his pilot pal, Des, the eager, bright-eyed ex-RAF type who'd taken us up for the somersault flight. I told Jeff it definitely wouldn't work. Des's short hair and unfashionable attire – hand-knitted pullovers, C&A trousers – would be an instant a no-no for style-conscious Rosemary. I was right. She was polite but aloof. Which meant our night out in the Star pub in St John's Wood Terrace ended on a somewhat sour note when we all walked back to the flat and Jeff and I, half-cut and overwhelmed as usual with lust, decided to noisily commandeer the tiny bedroom, leaving the other two staring at each other in the front room, waiting for us to hurry it all up and finish.

At one point, I introduced my new flatmate to a group of salesmen, mostly those I'd worked with at the electronics place. We'd regularly meet up for drinks in a pub off Charlotte Street. This revealed a somewhat surprising side to Rosemary. For despite her insistence on her relative purity, the one man she fell for was the last guy I'd expect her to be interested in: a petty criminal with gangland connections.

Each of the salesmen had a unique character, linked only by ducking and diving to make a fast buck. They included posh, well-spoken older men from Chelsea, suburban twits: former photocopier salesmen in cheap Burton or John Collier suits ('the window to watch,' the ad said, though few women would waste more than a passing glance at these guys), a couple of very good-looking out-of-work actors, shabby desperadoes in their sixties who had clearly hit hard times, Kent and South Coast chancers with various fiddles and sidelines. I met up with them because they were lively, humorous and good company, irrespective of their shady dealings.

Tony Connor made no secret of the fact that he'd done time, though it was never clear what for. Skinny, dark-haired and sardonic, he had a distinct aura of danger. You couldn't miss it – it shimmered off him. Disliked by the others because of his self-avowed prison past and because he didn't work much or bring in many sales, this man – the runt of the group in a way – was the one who held a curious fascination for my go-go dancing flatmate, despite all the other guys rushing to buy her drinks and get her attention for the briefest time. Odd, I thought. Why would she go for him?

Not long after introducing them, I came home from work to find a message on the answer machine: she must have given him the number. 'It's me, Tony. I'm gonna come round tomorrow night, Rosie. Be there, gal!'

I was fully expecting Rosemary to pull a face or laugh it off when she came home to the message; instead she amazed me. 'Oh, God! It's him! Are you out tomorrow night, Jacky? Aren't you seeing Jeff?'

I was, fortunately. The flat was far too small to entertain four people properly and anyway, Jeff shared the other salesmen's dislike of this guy. But romance will have its way. Very soon, I'd arrive home at night to find distinct traces of Tony's visits. An empty packet of Piccadilly cigarettes. A strong, all-pervasive smell of hashish. And a small, grayish white bandage that normally covered the stump that was his right thumb. He'd had most of it chopped off. Apparently the deed had been done by a henchman working for a gang of notorious south London criminals. An act of revenge, for God knows what.

I didn't know any of this thumb stuff until he started seeing Rosemary and told her this story. Bafflingly, he chose to reveal the stump to her during their smoking sessions. It was all quite bizarre. But what did genuinely amaze me was the Rosemary I was discovering. The faithful fiancée – waiting for the postman, working hard, diligently saving for her future – was now getting locked into something – I have no idea if it was fully consummated – with a sinister ex-con who made no bones about his criminal past. What would jealous, army man Mehmet, marching around in Turkey, have to say?

The dope-smoking didn't trouble me. I had no real interest in consuming any kind of drug or tobacco at that point. This was at a time when barbiturates and amphetamines were becoming widely used. Jacqueline Susann's book *Valley of the Dolls* – the story of three women in showbiz and their gradual dependence on uppers and downers – sold 30 million copies on its publication in 1966. Far from being put off by this tragic story highlighting the prevalence and problems of pill popping, more and more people started to take pills recreationally. Around that time NHS doctors were quite keen on legally prescribing a tranquilliser called Librium for anyone who claimed to be depressed and plenty of people I knew were openly popping such pills and happily offering them around. I did try them a couple of times and found them no fun at all – a dry mouth and feeling sleepy wasn't my idea of a wild time – but the drug culture was now making a real impact.

The wider influence of drug-taking came through the music industry as pop stars took drugs, got arrested and created huge headlines for their pains. Yet by the late '60s it wasn't only the wild boys of music, the Mick Jaggers and Keith Richards of this world, who were leading the way with their arrests and imprisonment for taking drugs. Beatle Paul McCartney freely admitted to millions of fans that he'd taken LSD, or acid as it is commonly known, bringing the idea of tripping on little tablets of hallucinogenic drugs out into the open. By the spring of 1968, women such as Judy Collins, a popular American singer, flew into London for concerts and TV appearances and happily told waiting press: 'I take drugs. I've smoked marijuana and I've taken LSD. I think marijuana should be legalised as quickly as possible.'

Millions of young people in Britain agreed. Teenagers in English seaside towns were getting hold of bits of hashish. Kids in the provinces were starting to puff away surreptitiously after school. Middle-class couples were lighting up with their friends at dinner parties. All this was, naturally, being reflected in the culture – not just in the big rock'n'roll world but in more mainstream music. Broadway musicals like *Hair* – a celebration of US hippie culture, the sexual revolution, drugs, racial harmony and the powerful opposition of young Americans to the Vietnam war (which had started in the 1950s but really escalated in the early to mid-1960s) – were also making headlines. *Hair*'s 'love is free' message – with nudity for the first time in a musical – had already taken US by storm and it opened in London in the autumn of 1968 to a roar of appreciation.

All around us, the word was out: sex, drugs and rock'n'roll were what mattered. Everything our parents stood for was old hat, passé. 'Tune in, turn on and drop out,' counter-culture guru Timothy Leary told an assembly of 30,000 very stoned San Francisco hippies in 1967. Essentially, this was translated into, 'Get stoned and if you've got any sense, give up the day job and do f★★★ all.' How could a generation like ours – raised in peacetime, jobs a-plenty, money in our pockets, with youthful role models who seemed as beautiful and in thrall to hedonism as anyone – ever hope to ignore such a call?

This call to out-and-out hedonism took a while to take effect. By the early '70s, smoking dope had virtually become *de rigueur* and people around me did start dropping out, quitting jobs, taking off, heading east. The hippie look – the beads, beards and long hair for men – started to be popular just before the end of the '60s, but the whole hippie culture was, in essence, a West Coast US phenomenon. Then it filtered into fashion, becoming a truly commercial thing: working kids could go out and buy hippie-style clothes – the Indian jackets, the brocade waistcoats, the flowing sleeves, snakeskin boots, fur boas – and play at being a stylish hippie on the weekend. That was part of the appeal.

Yet when it came to Rosemary, her attraction to the salesman and their shared love of ganja puzzled me. When she told me that he wrote poetry and would read it to her sometimes during their sessions, I was even more bemused by it all. A prison poet? There was, I figured, a sort of weird kind of romance in that: the bad boy lover trapped, yearning for freedom. Yet I was starting to see that her official line – the devoted fiancée – was a mere smoke screen (excuse the pun). There was quite a different Rosemary underneath.

Any doubts I might have had over Tony's notoriety were confirmed for me one summer's night. I'd hailed a taxi from the West End, rushing to the flat to get ready to go out. Almost home, we hit a bit of a traffic jam in Circus Road. My cab was briefly stationary. And there, some distance ahead of me, crossing the road at a zebra crossing, was Tony. It was too early for Rosemary to be home. He'd obviously tried, waited and decided to leave. But if he saw me, he'd want to come in. No way, I thought. 'Can't you move any faster?' I urged the cabby, diving down on the floor of the cab so Tony couldn't spot me. The cabbie turned round, looked at me in my ridiculous crouching position – not a great idea in a low-cut top and mini-skirt – and summed it all up with typical cabbies shrewdness.

'Nah, love. You fink I don't know Tony Connor ? Is 'e your bloke, then?'

Strangely enough, Jeff's initial dislike of Rosemary turned into full-on loathing once Tony was dropping in regularly. I'd get a heavy-duty diatribe if he came round and discovered they'd been smoking dope in the flat. 'He's an ex-con, Jacky. If the coppers find out about the dope, you'll get into trouble – it's your flat,' he'd remind me. 'It's disgusting.'

Why did he care? I thought it highly unlikely that a posse from the local police station would bother themselves about all this. At one point, I'd made a formal phone complaint to the local constabulary after encountering a man fully exposing himself to me and the deserted platform at St John's Wood tube station one morning, en route to work. (Flashers, for some reason, adored public transport at that time, long before the introduction of the CCTV cameras all over the place

halted the temptation to reveal their jewels to the world.)
A youngish copper had come round to the flat to discuss
it. Which promptly led to… er… did I fancy a drink
sometime? My attitude to the law was pretty much what
you'd expect from a Dalston-bred cynic with little respect
for authority. No way would I consider drinking with a
copper – cute or otherwise. Let alone anything else.

I didn't argue with Jeff about the dope-smoking
because I didn't care that much. But I thought he was
being a bit too, well, suburban about the whole thing.
Square. He came from a different world, really. He'd done
national service. He was a snazzy dresser – slick, lean
trousers, narrow three-button jacket, silky black roll-neck
top underneath – but his buddies were short-haired
business and yachting types who talked endless boy talk
about such things as sport and cars all the time. Their
wives probably had home perms by Toni or Twink and
wore drab dirndl skirts, I'd think to myself. These people
were probably harmless, decent people leading normal,
respectable lives. But I sneered, even looked down at the
suburban world of relative stability – so far away and
boring compared to the lives of two pelmet-skirted
blondes in St John's Wood, noisily banging the front door
behind us as we rushed out into Circus Road, leaping
into that night's date's waiting Mini Cooper or E type
Jag, whizzing down the road to a party with the little
Philips car record-player blasting 'A Day in the Life' or
'The Mighty Quinn'.

Our dedication to our appearance was considerable, though Rosemary's beauty routine was more advanced than mine. She'd use an infrared sun lamp, complete with little black goggles, to give her a faintly tanned look. (I tried it once but it was too strong for my pink, freckly skin.) She was also the first person I'd met to use the new, heated Carmen rollers. My focus was on getting the straight, blonde '60s babe look with the help of my cherished silky blonde hairpiece, purchased from Wig Wham in South Molton Street for five guineas. The piece had a mesh hair base that concealed a tiny little comb. The trick was to backcomb your hair and bury the comb in your hair by dragging the comb back. Then you'd pin it all in place and fiddle with it so that it all looked natural. It was tricky but it looked good. When it worked. My problem was that I didn't always anchor it properly because I was usually in such a hurry.

That year me and my hairpiece took a plane ride for our first trip to Majorca. I instantly fell for the pine-scented island and its sophisticated capital, Palma, drank cerveza in the bustling Plaza Gomila almost every night, and hooked up briefly with a handsome Irish singer called Danny who insisted on taking me to a club. He introduced me to his 'friend from Belfast', a dark-haired, dazzlingly good-looking young man we'd all been reading about. His name was George Best, El Beatle as he was dubbed. Everyone in the Palma nightclub – men and women alike – fawned over this new prince of football and an even vaster kingdom called 'celebrity', an ordinary lad from Northern Ireland catapulted way beyond anyone's wildest expectations when he joined Manchester United into something he could hardly be expected to understand. Or deal with.

Yet that night, smiling, calm, quietly acknowledging the fawners, the flatterers and the perfumed blondes, he seemed unconcerned, unfazed. Who knew then? For there, surrounded by booze and birds, his destiny for much of his life (when he wasn't on the pitch) was the first British football player elevated to the status of a pop star, a man for whom the '60s party never really stopped.

Something else takes place towards the end of the holiday in Majorca. It is an incredible coincidence arising from an innocent chat with a stranger, yet it leads to a startling discovery. The whole holiday has been a last-minute decision. Friends from my schooldays, Brenda and Kath, took a package deal to a posh, upmarket hotel just outside Palma. Kath is a laugh-a-minute, vivacious companion because her job, selling handbags in Bond Street's Gucci, gives her an endless stream of anecdotes about wealthy, often famous customers, mostly involving all sorts of crude passes made at her by rich older men. These, she claims, she always rejects. I tend to suspect otherwise. Booking much later, I manage to get a cheap deal to a nearby pension. This suits me fine, because I prefer not to hang out with them all the time – Kath's non-stop repertoire, while funny, can be exhausting – and I can use their hotel for sunbathing during the day.

It is there, beside the hotel pool in Palma Nova on the day before the holiday ends, dangling my toes in the water, I find myself chatting to a pleasant older woman. She says she hails from Guildford, Surrey. 'And where do you live?' she wants to know, after I've told her I'm from London and work as a shoe chain store secretary-cum-complaints manager.

'Oh, I've got a flat in St John's Wood,' I reply. 'I share with another girl.' The woman's curiosity, never far from the surface, is now instantly piqued, I can see. Flat-sharing isn't unknown. But at that point, with all the noise around swinging London, it probably all seems quite exotic to her.

'So who do you flat-share with, then?' asks Mrs Nosey. 'Is she a secretary as well?'

'Oh, a girl called Rosemary Smart. She manages an employment agency. She's from Surrey, too. I think she's from Guildford,' I add helpfully.

The woman looks at me. Her eyes narrow. She cranes her blonde bouffant head forward. 'Rosemary Smart? Fair hair, very thin, went to live abroad?'

'Yes, that's her. How amazing. You know her!'

'Oh, everyone in the area knows Rosemary. The family. They used to have a sweet shop. Now she's got a kid, a little girl. She had her when she was 18. The parents bring her up.'

'No, you must be mistaken,' I tell the woman. 'I live with her. She's never mentioned any little girl. Or a sweet shop. It can't be her.'

'Oh, I think it is,' says Mrs Nosey, getting up from her chair, picking up her bag and towel and readying herself to move into the shade. 'You'd better ask her. That child doesn't even know she's her mum. They've told her she's her sister. Terrible, isn't it?' And with that, she just walks away, her bullets fired, leaving me stunned.

My mind is racing. Surely it can't be true? Can it? Yet the more I think about it, the more the pieces of the jigsaw start to fit. The apparent lack of interest in sex. Her somewhat shaky pose as a virginal innocent – she's never once admitted to me that she's slept with anyone. Her dismay at my admission about the pill. And the way that she keeps her family and her life in London entirely separate – the weekend trips 'home' she never ever discusses. My mum rings the flat sometimes for a chat but Rosemary has never had a call or a message from 'home' since we've lived there. The go-go dancer in Istanbul remained there for two years because she needed or wanted to get away from her truth: she's an unmarried mum of a small girl. Yet to most of the world, she's a secret. She doesn't quite exist. It's a lot to take in. Curiously, for once, I say nothing to anyone about this surprising conversation.

On the plane going back, I think I can see why she's deployed this subterfuge. She'd have fallen pregnant earlier in the '60s, before the pill, before the abortion laws changed. She'd probably had no choice: a teenage girl who had been caught out by a single act and was trapped by the harsh social attitudes towards illegitimacy, attitudes that were starting to change now but too late for her. A secret it was and so it remained. Who knows what happened to the girl's father? Maybe he'd done a runner? That could easily have happened. Or maybe her parents didn't like him and didn't want a marriage. I struggle with it all. I flash back to that awful day in the Dalston doctor's surgery, his disapproval of me and I understand all too well what she'd been up against. Financially, her parents had taken over, lent their support – as I'm sure some families did sometimes.

Certainly, whatever she did, she couldn't win. Had she kept the girl, remained with her parents at home and brought her up, they would have all faced local whispers and sniggers – as would her child once she was at school. Handing her over to strangers for adoption was obviously not an option. Yet this way, letting her parents take over, she was still open to criticism for being an uncaring, unloving mother. I do get it – well, most of it. But what I can't get over, for some reason, is the fact that the little girl is a secret. Her own child, unacknowledged as such to the wider world. I know why this has all happened but I can't come to terms with how she accommodates it – how she can live a lie all the time. OK, she'd gone off for a couple of years, hidden herself away. But now, if what I'd been told was right, she was willing to continue the charade, not even tell the small girl the truth. That to me is enormous, a deception too far, though I could hardly have understood what it meant to have your baby, then let your parents take over. Yet as I run through the story of Rosemary's baby, if you'll forgive the cliché, I suddenly remember what Jeff had noticed. He'd spotted a millisecond of a truth withheld, a subterfuge that dominated several lives.

Can I carry on living with her, knowing the truth behind the façade? Or do I step forward and confront her with what I'd heard? In the end, I opt to say nothing, keep it to myself. For now, at least.

CHAPTER SIX

AN UNRAVELLING

A small, dark furry creature nuzzles up against me, purring as I lug my suitcase through the front door. A feline house guest. Sure enough, there's a note on my bed from Rosemary. 'Looks like we've solved the mouse problem,' she writes, informing me she's taken a week off work to visit her parents.

There's also a really odd message from Jeff on the answering machine. 'Hope you had a good time, gorgeous. Guess what? I'm going sailing with Kevin on his new 30-footer. We're heading for France. Save your suntan for me, lovely!' This is unusual, sets me worrying. Jeff never leaves messages on the machine. He just rings me at work. If I'm not around, he calls back until he gets me. Something's definitely wrong.

At least the cat sticks around, vanishing briefly then

reappearing intermittently through that autumn. At one point, I even start to leave food out, though I never bother to name our pet-from-nowhere, to which I become curiously attached. I'm preoccupied, mostly, with the absence of any action from Jeff. I don't hear from him for three weeks after that message. When I do, he insists persuasively he's had all sorts of things going on and do I want to come sailing that weekend? I go and it's a ghastly idea. Love in a cramped, damp cabin, bobbing about on the chilly English Channel, is not a success. I am irritated and bitchy: mostly, he pretends not to notice.

After our time on the boat, communication gaps widen further. Weeks turn into months until he contacts me, always with some disarming story that I want to believe, but don't. When a relationship starts to crumble, you hang on in there, even though the really good times are already consigned to history. There are tantrums and tears when I do see him. I accuse him of infidelity, lying and keeping secrets. He denies, evades, brushes it all off, soothes me temporarily with affection, cuddles – though he's not so quick to rush me into bed any more and, of course, I won't ever make the first move, I'm so used to being wooed.

Out of habit, I distract myself, out most nights, as is Rosemary who has mysteriously acquired a couple of portly, cigar chomping, well-heeled admirers, older married men 'in property' driving around in Jaguars and Humber Super Snipes. They like having her on their arm for dinner and cabaret at expensive places like the Talk of the Town in Leicester Square or the Top of the Tower, the revolving restaurant in the newly opened Post Office Tower. There they can eat expensive meals 34 floors up, items such as caviar and huge steaks. Or they take her for meals at the big West End hotels and drop her off early, which seems to please her.

In an attempt to stop worrying about Jeff I have what is essentially a three-date fling with Dave, a good-looking Carnaby Street shop owner. It ends once we finally get down to it, a deeply unsatisfactory experience, all over in a flash. Never again. Especially since Rosemary arrives home early and catches us at it on the kitchen floor. 'All I could see was his bum going up and down!' she chortles the next morning.

A few weeks later, at a South Ken party I collide with a jaw-droppingly handsome 20-something Iranian, Saeed. Iranians were called Persians then and there seemed to be many in London, rich playboys subsidised by their dads, ostensibly studying but spending all their time gambling and girling and living in splendour in centrally heated flats. Central heating was still a bit of a luxury back then (less than 30 per cent of UK homes boasted a central heating system). Saeed didn't drink or smoke dope. He'd never even been inside a London pub. Yet he was, beyond any doubt, a love god in the looks stakes (imagine a youthful version of the cricketing Imran Kahn), hence my willingness to stay over at his plushly carpeted, heated pad in South Ken. It has to be said, though, while he wasn't a never-again disaster like Carnaby Street Dave, his lovemaking skills were pretty average. Vanilla.

That final year of the '60s started with a nasty, cold London winter. Snow. Slush. My enthusiasm for my job at the shoe firm had waned too – but it was far too miserable out there to consider a trek round the agencies to hunt for something else. There were forlorn nights that winter when I remained huddled over the two-bar electric heater in the damp, dank flat with only the cat for company until Rosemary, svelte and warm in her expensive fox-fur jacket and high leather boots, blonde hair streaming behind her, would come home from one of her early dinner dates in triumph. She would report a juicy steak *au poivre* at Le Cellier du Midi up in Hampstead and 'not even a peck on the cheek' for the bewitched, wedlocked property mogul. This seemed to be a satisfying experience for her in curious ways I could never quite figure. I know her secret. But definitely not the woman.

One night, she greets me after work, waving a blue airmail letter with a Turkish stamp. 'Mehmet's got a friend who's coming over next week. He owns a nightclub in Istanbul so he'll want to go out on the town. Can you come with us, Jacky? He wants to have a good time and I've promised Mehmet I'll show him around.'

I've never met anyone from Turkey before. In truth, I

just about know where Turkey is, mostly thanks to the old song 'Istanbul not Constantinople'. Sometimes you'd see very odd advertisements in the *Standard* for salespeople to sell 'luxury goods' in Turkey and the Far East, no languages needed. Which did make you wonder: did everyone there speak English? But as far as a night on the town went, why ever not?

A week later, two 30-something men in smartly tailored three-piece suits, white shirts, neat little ties and unfashionably short dark hair, are at our front door, fully primed to escort two swinging London dolly birds around town. The nightclub owner, Huseyin, speaks not a single word of English. He's not gross – he's quite pleasant – but we can't communicate, which is just as well since I find him deeply unfanciable. The other one, however, is different. Ahmet, who has lived in London for many years, is short but very good-looking – and extremely charming. He reeks of Brut aftershave which by the mid-'60s had knocked Old Spice off its perch as the leading aftershave brand available to men hoping to enhance their allure.

We take a taxi to the Playboy club, the place Huseyin is desperate to visit. It opened to great fanfare in Park Lane in 1966 and it's still very much a novelty, with the Bunny Girls serving at the tables in their extremely provocative, specially-fitted outfits (boob-squeezing satin corset, dark tights, high heels and the awful bunny ears and bushy white tail on the derriere) and the reputation of Playboy, with its famous men's magazine and string of clubs all over the US. But it is really the London Playboy casino that is the main draw – and which will go on to rake in the millions for owner Hugh Hefner and his first foray into Europe.

I'm curious to have a look, of course, but have no interest whatsoever in gambling (a permanent hangover from my dad's bookie world and disastrous fall from grace). I decide it's a place that merits just one visit. Despite all the newspaper hype, once seated at our table with drinks and indifferently prepared meals served by a series of smiling, pert Bunnies (how can they breathe in those corsets?), it seems pretty charmless, a shallow, bland way of – well, selling the idea of a love-in with a good-looking woman already packaged for a man's delight. There are strict and well publicised rules about the Bunny girls not being able to consort with the customers afterwards (look but don't touch – oh, yeah?). Funnily enough, the Bunnies themselves eventually move with the times and by the mid-1970s they will join the merry-go-round of the militant trade unions and go on strike. But the overall initial impression that night is of plasticised, packaged sex not quite for sale. It's quite different from today's raunchy hen nights, with muscular male strippers being hauled off by over-amorous females for not so discreet personal services.

The following night, the Turks whisk us to Park Lane again, this time to Trader Vic's Polynesian-themed bar in the newly built Hilton Hotel, very much one of London's smartest, upmarket venues. Trader Vic's was an expensive, special occasion place, a big Saturday night make-an-impression date haunt, quite different to the tiny, dark bistros with gingham tablecloths (menu: prawn cocktail followed by Steak Diane) or local Indian restaurants I was accustomed to. After our session at Trader Vic's and a couple of luridly coloured cocktails with tiny flags on sticks, Ahmet, who seems to know every doorman or manager wherever we go, suggests we dine at the Lotus House, an expensive and popular Chinese restaurant, one of the first big London eateries to do expensive takeaway deliveries around town. By now, Rosemary is nudging me towards the nightclub owner, for reasons only known to her.

'He really likes you,' she told me excitedly after the first date. 'Ahmet rang me at work today and told me. He wants you to come out to Turkey for a holiday as his guest. It'll all be above board. He'll pay your fare and everything. You'll stay at the best hotel at Istanbul. As long as you want. If you like, he'll take you shopping, buy you new clothes.'

'I'm not interested,' I snap and it's the truth. Beyond the Brut and the expensive meals, I detect a whiff of… something extremely dodgy. The words 'white slave trade' flash up in big letters in my head. Ahmet had become very pally on the second date, but in a sneaky way. Whenever Rosemary would disappear to the loo,

121

he'd start chatting me up furiously, knowing his friend couldn't understand a word. 'Where you work?' he demands. 'I pick you up from your office one day after Huseyin goes back.' No, I assure him, I prefer to come home straight after work. No need to visit my office.

After one more night out as a foursome, this time to a big London Steak House in Kensington High Street, Huseyin leaves town. He says goodbye with a big smile, burbling in Turkish to Ahmet, who translates. 'He says he hopes very much that you will come to Istanbul as his guest,' he tells me. 'He says you are a beautiful lady and he would be proud to show you his city.' It all sounds like bullshit to me. What's that saying about a rubbish deal? If it sounds too good to be true, it probably is. Later, as we settle into our creaky single beds, I tell Rosemary exactly what I think.

'It's so obvious. Get an English girl there, promise her the moon – and then what? Lock you up in a flat and send their mates round? They must think I'm daft if they believe I'd go there.'

'Oh, no, Jacky. They mean it, they're perfect gentlemen,' my flatmate assures me. 'Mehmet knows them very well. You wouldn't be in any danger if you went there. He just wanted them to see me, make sure I'm OK – and not *doing anything*.' There she goes again, pretending to be swinging London's last remaining virgin. I'm snoring my head off within minutes. I can no longer trust a single word she says and I'm quite capable of making my own decisions anyway. My instincts are sound.

Yet just a couple of weeks later, when I get an unexpected phone call at work from Ahmet, asking if I'll see him on Saturday night, I make a huge blunder. I go. There's still a big Jeff-sized gap in my life and it's one of Rosemary's weekends in Guildford. He drives me – in his very racy cream-coloured Alfa Romeo – to a beautiful restaurant on the Thames, quite a long way out of London. He talks endlessly of Istanbul, how beautiful it is, how warm, how so many young women like me go there, love it. He's planning to drive there soon. It would take a few days but it would be a lovely holiday. Come with me, he says beguilingly over the rum baba I'm greedily forking for my dessert.

'No,' I tell him. 'I can't. I've had my holiday this year.' He seems to accept this but then, on the drive back, he silkily suggests we stop off at a nearby waterside hotel for the night. 'No, thanks,' I tell him. I have not, for some reason, seen this coming, focusing only on the event itself. I don't perceive myself as an acquisitive woman, but nevertheless I have the expectation that it is my right to be wined and dined by any prospective suitor, regardless if I fancy them or not.

'Why?' he wants to know. 'You look like you like me: I can tell.'

'Oh, I like you but I've got a boyfriend,' I inform him smugly.

He ignores this. He isn't going to give up that easily. 'It's Rosemary. You don't want her to know you like me. You think she like me, don't you?'

Oh, God. Will he just shut it? Finally, we're in St John's Wood. Merciful escape ahead. As he pulls the car up outside the flat, an irrational, stupid impulse takes over. I dive into my handbag. 'Look,' I tell him, producing a crumpled Polaroid of Jeff I've kept there for some reason. I shove it right under his nose. This'll get the message through. 'This is my boyfriend. I sleep with him, no one else.'

Big, big blunder. Red rag to a bull. He flicks the photo away and I dive to retrieve it.

'Hah! Your boyfriend! I fuck him, the Englishman!' I'm not quite expecting the idea of him fucking my fast-disappearing Brit bloke. It's a disturbing image.

Shocked, I reach for the handle of the car door. But he's faster than me. Ahmet grabs me, tries to force me into a kiss, and while I manage to wriggle away, avert my head in the confined space, there's a nasty, short, feverish tussle. Heaven knows how I do it but I somehow release the door handle and with one final, angry gesture as I leave the car, he reaches out, grabs my hair, tugs – and oh, the shame – the perilously constructed edifice that is my big blonde hairdo falls apart. The hairpiece flies off. I stumble out, dishevelled and humiliated, into the night, onto the pavement, my false hairpiece now lying in disgrace near my front door. Goodbye, blondie. Hello, dirty brown roots. As a lucky afterthought, he leans forward, chucks my precious quilted Chanel bag into the gutter – and screeches off with all speed.

It's horrible. He hasn't hurt me. And it could have been so much worse had we not been in a parked car outside my flat. I'm pretty sure he could have tried to rape me. But the humiliation, the dislodgement of my hairpiece, lying there on the pavement like an abandoned kipper, are quite enough. And the comment about fucking an Englishman has rattled me no end. I've known about homosexuality since I was a kid. My dad would always take the piss out of the male dancers on the telly. 'Ooh, look at the nancy boys,' he'd say in affected mimicry, so typical of the prejudices of his era and his background. But at this point, I had never considered the idea that a man who'd invite me into bed would also think about bedding a man. Bisexuality was not a word you heard openly bandied around then. I totter upstairs, collapse on my bed. What were these guys like?

The next morning, the phone rings at 7 am, waking me through the paper-thin partition wall. I don't pick up. It's Ahmet. He leaves a message. He's really sorry, he shouldn't have done that. 'Please forgive me, Jacky,' he's saying. 'I didn't mean any harm.'
Oh really? Then, it starts to sink in. Now, I start to get it – well, some of it. The 'fuck the Englishman' is still fresh in my mind. I figure he was trying to keep me sweet – perhaps by sleeping with me as a softening-up ploy? – for

the other guy, the nightclub boss. Essentially, he's a pimp, a procurer. It was clear there was some sort of financial relationship between the two men. I'd already noticed that he acted more like a gofer around him than a friend. And nightclub man Huseyin had paid for everything with noticeably thick wads of cash. Now, of course, Ahmet's blown it. No nooky for him but much worse, no Jacky for nightclub man either.

That Sunday I stay at home, only running out across the road briefly to Panzer to buy Nimble bread ('slice for slice, fewer calories than ordinary bread') and Italian salami Milano (an odd breakfast but one which sustains me through many years of hangovers). The phone rings continuously every hour, on the hour. But there are no more messages. And Rosemary doesn't return that night: she's obviously going straight to work from Surrey on Monday morning.

At work I'm off-kilter, my equilibrium shaken by all the things that have been running through my mind and the realisation that I don't always know the score with men. My boss is off at some big sporting event, the level of complaints has temporarily tailed off so I'm more or less left to my own devices. What was I doing? Why was I pretending to myself that Jeff was my boyfriend when I hardly saw him, never knew what he was up to? And then I do something I should have done months ago: I dial Jeff's office number and instead of merely mumbling my thanks when told he's not there, I scream at the smug girl answering the phone: 'You tell Jeff to bloody ring me – or I'm coming down there!' I know where the office is. It's in Kilburn. Ages ago, I got the address, sneaking one of Jeff's business cards from his wallet and writing it down when he was sleeping on the boat.

Lunch time. No call comes through. Action. I hail a black cab outside the office and head for Kilburn. Then, from a red call box, I ring Jeff's office again. This time, he picks up. He's expecting something like this. OK, he says somewhat soberly, meet me in the car park at the back of the office building. And there, in the office car park, Jeff, immaculate in his smart grey suit from Cue, stands there and reveals the truth. All of it. He's lived, on and off, with a widow in Pinner in her semi for several years. They go back a long way. She was the best friend of a girl he'd got into trouble when he was much younger. He still went up to see the boy in Scotland every year, but there was no relationship with the boy's mum. It had started to go wrong with Mrs Pinner long before he met me. But whenever he said he wanted to leave, she'd gone potty, so he'd hung on. And then… well, he loved me. I knew that, didn't I? But once he'd started the new company, he'd fallen hard for his secretary, Maureen (the smug girl taking my calls). And now he'd left Pinner and moved in with Maureen. Into her flat.

Yes, he was truly sorry. He should have done something about it before. But he had too much going on, what with work and the sailing. 'Anyway, Jack, you've still got it all going for you, haven't you? You've got a great job, a flat – and you're gorgeous, anyway!'

Typical Jeff. Brush aside all negatives. Flatter like crazy. The reality was: work alongside randy, raunchy Jeff and you had his attention and his body. Later I discovered from one of his other conquests that I was far from the only girl in the office that he'd shagged. What narked me was that smug Maureen had somehow got him to move on. But in truth, I'd never tried or aimed for that, had I? I'd just gone along for the ride.

I am quite stunned at this betrayal. Back in my cubbyhole at work, my typewriter littered with scribbled notes to ring angry customers, I try my best to analyse it all. I hadn't been faithful, had I? So what did I expect? I could see he was a bit of a lecher when I met him. Yet I allowed myself to be seduced by – an experienced seducer. There was no logic to any of it. Perhaps I'd clung to the idea of the relationship rather than the reality for too long. Until the penny dropped.

Isn't it funny how in life, if one thing goes badly wrong, there's sure to be another disaster hot on its heels? That same night, I get back to the flat to find a somewhat puzzled Rosemary. An enormous bouquet of red roses has been delivered that afternoon, left on our doorstep, addressed to me. The card attached says: 'Sorry, Jacky. Let me make it up to you, love and kisses, Ahmet.'

'What's going on?' Rosemary wants to know. I can see by her expression she's really narked that he's sent them to me – not her. The ego of this woman, her duplicity and delight at winding men up: it's just too much for me. I don't bother to fill her in on the story of the hairpiece and the tussle. Probably because of my distress about Jeff, all my anger and frustration flies out, in a torrent of abuse. I let rip. Completely. Mine own executioner, really… what the fuck is she doing, pairing me off with those tossers? Anyone can see what they were doing, trying to get me to Istanbul, so they can do God knows what. And what's all this crap about being faithful to Mehmet when she's having it off with Mr Thumb-less? Does she think I'm stupid?

Wrong choice of words as usual.

'I've never slept with him!' Rosemary screams at the top of her voice. 'I want to be with Mehmet, he really loves me!'

'Oh yeah, and what about your *kid*!' I screech in ghastly retort. 'You've got a bloody *kid* – and no one knows she exists!'

She stares at me, wild-eyed. For a nanosecond, I think she's going thump me. But she doesn't. Nonetheless, it's an ugly verbal equivalent of a hideous, hair-tugging, rolling on the floor, girly catfight. 'My parents have adopted her!' she screams at the top of her voice. 'And what about you? *You're on the pill*! You sleep with *anyone*! I bet your mother would be pleased to hear that!'

Sounds daft now, doesn't it? But that's how it was: illegitimacy, birth control for single women, multiple lovers – still a mark of shame according to a lot of people. Even in London in the spring of 1969.

The little flat with its flimsy walls is now far too small for two young women who have reached such a nadir in their relationship that even one more night in the same room is too much. All that remains is sterile, chilly silence. Rosemary packs her bags immediately, rings a faithful slave in yet another flash car who drives her off to the station and a return to Surrey. I have a week left at the flat to contact the landlord, hand in our notice and find another place to live.

In the space of just 24 hours, everything has unravelled. Amazingly, I'd held back for months from spilling the beans to Rosemary. But it's not in my nature to keep my thoughts to myself permanently. As for Jeff, I should have followed my early instincts, at least made some attempt to protect myself emotionally. But while I was having such a good time with him, it was easier and far more exciting to focus on the more basic ones…

Did this fiasco with Jeff harden my heart, help me wise up, make me more wary in my choices in the future? The truth is, it didn't change anything at all. It sent me spiralling downward briefly. But not for long. Remember the yo-yo craze? The yo-yo was big in the early '60s and even made a comeback in popularity in the 1980s. That best describes me as a 20-something: a human yo-yo. Down I'd go on the string, hitting the lows emotionally, usually over a romance, only to bounce back up again for the highs (the next romance), repeating exactly the same exercise again and again.

My mum, Molly, once summed it up perfectly: 'You're a bouncing ball, Jack.' Yes, there is some merit in refusing to stay down for too long. But, oh, what an emotionally seesawing time it is when you opt for a prolonged, protracted youth with only freedom as your beacon. Because at this point, my heady pursuit of sexual experience, momentary excitement and whatever else the changing times had to offer, was very far from running out of steam. Ahead of me were more detours and disasters, yet nothing would bring me to a halt. Even though I was constantly hurtling towards a destination I couldn't name, searching for an identity I couldn't define.

I knew what I didn't want: stability, respectability, leading a planned, ordinary but safe life with a steady, sensible man. These things were fine for other people. But I was in a changing world, living in the city right in the middle of it all, the happening place. Tears today – but an unknown tomorrow. The challenge of the unknown would always release me from any hurt, self-inflicted or otherwise.

So I threw away my hairpiece, packed my bags and set off for uncharted territory, a female Dick Whittington without a compass. The enormous bouquet of red roses was left, unwrapped and ignored, by the dirty crockery on the side of the kitchen sink. I didn't even trouble myself to chuck them in the bin.

CHAPTER SEVEN
THE '60S ARE OVER

A large house on Islington's Liverpool Road where a New Year's Eve party is in full swing. People drift from room to room, voices increasingly louder, the sound of The Archies singing 'Sugar Sugar' almost drowned out by the burble of chatter, the intermittent outbreaks of loud, raucous laughter, the anticipation of Big Ben's chime half an hour away. No one dances. Not yet.

A faint odour of hashish mingles with the more powerful scent of patchouli oil, the exotic, musky late '60s hippie smell. The hosts, a married couple – he an ad agency boss, she something in fashion – are an effusive, outgoing, late 20-something pair. Rumour has it he's having it off with his secretary. And that she too has flirtatious, messy liaisons. Welcome to the dawn of the 1970s…

I'm perched on a low, extremely uncomfortable orange chair from a shop called Habitat, wondering where Michael has suddenly vanished to. These are his friends, his advertising crowd from work. Big pine table in the kitchen, shag pile rugs, chrome and glass furniture in the living area. Even a sofa made out of dark leather. I have never seen furniture like this before, other than in photos in the posh Sunday supplements. I feel a bit out of my depth, mainly because I know no one here. Where is he?

Michael is the love of my life. We've been together for several months, the first few living *a deux* in Highgate, wrapped up in each other to the exclusion of most of the world. He's gentle, soulful and sensitive, a talented art director with an unhappy, long-term relationship behind him. Curly, unruly brown hair, piercing blue eyes. Michael often insists he'd be happier as a dreamy, itinerant hippie on Ibiza if he didn't have to earn a living, pay his way in the world. He's a guitarist, sings beautifully and serenades me with songs like 'Lay Lady Lay', the sexy Bob Dylan hit. He's gently humorous – he teases me endearingly about my fixations, my onion-style upswept hairdos and see-through lacy outfits. He's knowledgeable about art and classical music, in an unpretentious way.

Michael is a new world for me. This is no frenetic, sexually charged headlong dive into pleasure with an experienced seducer. Love with this man means just that, a softly melting fusion, two people fitting together perfectly, lovingly, completely in synch. So familiar is he to my senses, it's almost as if we've known each other before – in another life. Michael, for me, is a place of total harmony, blissful contentment. The rest of the world can go hang. Snuggling up to his long, lean shape each night, waking with his arms wrapped tightly round me, finding myself adrift in endless warmth and affection for the first time ever, I'm blissfully in love and it's a two-way street. He tells me how he cares and shows me he adores me in a thousand ways. Not by lavishing me with expensive gifts or taking me to flash places. But by small, unexpected gestures – like leaving tiny, folded up love notes for me in my handbag. I still remember them: 'Jacqui of a thousand delights. I'll be at work when you wake up. But I'll be thinking all day long about your soft, delicious skin…'

He'd been born in Scotland but moved south with his parents as a toddler. We'd been introduced in a pub by a mutual friend, a copywriter who'd worked with him. At that point, I was temping in an extremely dull solicitor's office off Rosebery Avenue. I'd quit the shoe firm just after leaving Circus Road and taken a series of dreary two-week temp bookings to keep going through the last summer of the '60s.

Moving from Circus Road that spring had been relatively painless. With the help of a friend of a friend who knew someone – I didn't trust ads any more – I'd swiftly found a new place in the same area: up on the 20th floor of a brand new, high-rise council block in Abbey Road, a ten-minute walk from the zebra crossing where, that very summer, the Fab Four strode across the street, John leading the way in his beautiful white suit, as they crossed into musical history with their last album together.

The Abbey Road block had more than a hundred flats of different sizes but I was in a one-bedder. Not a great idea. The tenant, Sheila, believed she could let out the bedroom to me (for a fiver a week) and sleep on the living-room couch. This was fine until her giant of a boyfriend, singing in the chorus of a West End show, came to stay each weekend and I couldn't get into the bathroom in the mornings. It really wasn't an ideal situation, though at least the view across London was spectacular. The novelty of newly built, high-rise living was quite a thrill for me – there was even a state of the art waste-disposal unit in the kitchen sink, a far cry from the smelly rubbish chute I'd lived with in my Dalston days – though at the time many people shunned and distrusted these new, high-rise council buildings. They didn't exactly have a great reputation after the near-collapse, in 1968, of Ronan Point, a new 22-storey tower block in east London. Two people had died in a gas explosion there. One of my friends, Laurie – he of the ashtray-chucking – wouldn't venture into the lift of my new place, let alone come up 22 floors. Yet within a couple of years he would buy his first flat on the top floor of... a high rise.

I must have been there for about three months when I met Michael, by which time I had at last stopped thinking about Jeff's betrayal and understood it for what it was: a hot affair with a Bad Boy. I never saw Jeff or Rosemary ever again. That chapter was closed for good. But at the same time I had decided to stay away from men and such entanglements for a while and to remain truly free in every way. Until that night in a crowded pub in Seven Dials in Covent Garden, surrounded by long-haired, young advertising art directors and copywriters in flowered shirts and fat kipper ties. We were drawn to each other immediately. Yet it wasn't Michael's sexual allure or charisma that created the instant magnetism, more a recognition that here was a kind, gentle, loving man, an artistic person, someone to be totally at ease with, learn from. Hours later, arms wrapped round each other, we left the heaving, packed pub and went off to his Highgate flat that first night – and that was it.

I stopped temping. I just stayed in the flat, waiting for Michael to come home from work at night. There was, of course, no attempt at domesticity, playing the little woman. The flat was big and in a pretty, tree-lined road – but it was barely furnished and rundown. More mice in the kitchen, damp patches on the ceiling, a greedy gas meter you had to constantly feed with coins if you wanted to stay warm. Mostly, we'd go to the nearest pub for drinks (glasses of Mateus Rosé for me, Skol lager or brown ale for Michael) and sustenance (more cheese rolls). If I went into town to meet him from the office we would eat pasta in Soho dives like the Amalfi on Old Compton Street. It didn't trouble me that I didn't work, though it did seem to bother others. 'But what will happen if you run out of money?' one puzzled girlfriend asked me. I'd shrug. Michael earned good money and he wasn't stingy. That bridge would be crossed if and when we came to it. Right now my sole responsibility was to be with him, 24/7.

Molly and Ginger were frantic with worry when I rang from a phone box and told them I was living in Michael's flat. About a week later, they even turned up at the front door – foolishly I'd given them the address to placate them, as there was no phone. They stood there in the draughty hallway – Ginger, portly in his immaculate, three-piece suit from Hector Powe, Molly equally smart in her Julius wool coat, virtually pleading with me to come back to Dalston. I was appalled that they'd do this, turning up to give way to their feelings. What did they think? I was a woman of 25, living with a man. So what? But for their generation, 'living in sin' was a no-no, one of many ridiculous conventions like expecting me to stay put at home, waiting for Mr Right to deliver me into a life of suburban conformity. I shouldn't have been so open about it and told them what I was doing, of course. But I'd figured they'd just have to accept it. I knew my dad's possessive attitude made life hellish for my mum sometimes. He'd been the one to drag her here. Quite a few girls I knew were in situations that earlier generations found socially unacceptable – and I had sometimes discussed these with Molly who hadn't seemed particularly unnerved by my friends' stories.

Two of my single 20-something friends had gone off, on their own, to live abroad, one to the USA, another to work as a courier for a travel firm. Another girlfriend had a long-term, married boyfriend who was about to divorce his wife now that huge changes to the divorce laws were coming through. The 1969 Divorce Law Reform Act came into effect in 1971 and made it much easier for couples to divorce. It would change millions of lives and wipe out, once and for all, the lingering stigma around divorce that had persisted beyond the 1950s.

'We're your parents,' said Ginger. 'You've gotta respect us.'

Then Molly started to weep. 'What did we do to make you do this, Jac? Why?'

Michael stood in the hallway, his arm protectively round me. But he said little. 'Jacky's fine here with me,' he told them quietly. I was glad he didn't try to intervene or take my dad on. Fortunately, there was a taxi waiting for my parents outside the house, its meter still running. Ginger no longer lived his bookie life of Riley, but had retained his loyalty to the black cab. I didn't have to say 'Piss off', but there was nothing more they could say or do. They left, Molly still dabbing her eyes with her hanky.

And no, I didn't feel bad. Just angry that they'd done this. It had been a futile exercise.

'You're well out of that, Jacky,' was Michael's only comment as the cab drove off.

I'd already told him everything about me, so he understood it all. Yet as romantic as it all was, just the two of us, eventually the real world crept in. Michael was offered a new job with heaps more money than he was earning. The drawback was that it was in Holland. The Dutch were dead keen to recruit art directors from trendy London agencies but only a few people were prepared to leave the swinging city, so the Dutch had to up the ante. But my initial dismay at this news didn't last for long: there was a middle way. 'I'll fly back every Friday and we can have weekends together,' Michael assured me. 'The only problem is, we have to get out of the flat. The landlady wants it back for her son.'

So that was how I went back to temping for Office Overload (at 12 shillings an hour) and moved yet again, this time into a small ground-floor bedsit in Woodland Gardens, off the long Muswell Hill Road, priced at £6 a week, with a bathroom to myself on the landing. It seemed like a good solution: we'd split the rent, I'd get my privacy again and we'd have all our weekends together. Yet the very first weekend he came back, Michael told me he didn't like the new job. The people he was working with were cold, unfriendly. He missed me, he missed London and they wanted him to work late sometimes on Fridays – meaning he wouldn't always be able to get the last flight into London. So our perfect weekends together – staying mostly in bed, listening to Astrud Gilberto's 1965 album *Look for the Rainbow* on Michael's portable player, eating tinned Campbell's soup heated on the tiny gas ring, going for the occasional walk in Highgate Woods – were sometimes cancelled at the eleventh hour. Thankfully, he'd got a week's holiday off after Christmas. At least we'd be seeing in 1970 together, I thought. Yet in the same way that all the optimism and bright energy of the '60s somehow faded with the onset of the darker, grimmer '70s, so my love affair changed direction that very New Year's Eve.

As midnight approaches the Islington party is more crowded, more raucous. But where is Michael? I wander into every room, look upstairs, but all I find are laughing, joking, well-oiled or stoned revellers and a kitchen strewn with empty bottles of Pale Ale and Babycham, the usual mad crush you find at any packed New Year's bash. The front door to the house is wide open. I step outside and there he is. My love is sitting there on the cold, cold grass, crying, his tie askew, his new corduroy jacket crumpled, pink shirt unbuttoned and half hanging out of his trousers. He is sobbing his heart out, his head in his hands. What's going on? I run over, throw my arms round him, desperate to comfort him. I've never seen him like this before.

'What's wrong, Mike? What's happened? Tell me what's wrong!' I plead.

Michael merely pushes me away. Then he looks at me, the tears still trickling down his face and I realise I'm looking at a totally different person. He now looks quite wild-eyed and deranged. In fact, he's looking at me as if I'm a hateful stranger. '*You*! You knew! You knew they were laughing at me! They hate me! Every one of them hates me!'

What is all this about? I have no idea what is happening. He was fine when we got here about an hour or so back. What's changed? In all the time we've spent together, I've never once seen Michael get angry, lose his temper or shout. In fact it's one of the things I love about him. I know he's quite shy around other people – he's told me that many times. This is the first time we've even gone to a party together. But who is this person ranting and raving before me? And why would anyone hate him? Yet before I can say another word, he's gone. He's running away, a dishevelled figure flying down the Essex Road, out into the night. I stand there, rooted to the spot. I really don't know what to do. I'm totally bewildered. Stunned. Part of me wants to go after him, the other thinks it's best to stay put, try and make sense of it all. But there is no sense to any of this. Something is very, very wrong with Michael and I have no idea what it is or how to reach out to him, help him. I go inside, don my long black maxi coat, pick up my shoulder bag and hastily say farewell to my hosts, who are now oblivious to everything but the heady, sweaty momentum of their party.

At the stroke of midnight, the dawn of 1970, I'm on the street, trying to hail a cab. Impossible. I wait, I walk and eventually, after about half an hour, a cab drops a noisy group off and I head for Muswell Hill, hoping he'll be there to greet me. He's not there. I lie wide awake for hours but he doesn't come back. I finally doze off at about 6 am. His things are here, I tell myself repeatedly. He has to come back. Later, I open his small suitcase. Inside are clothes, neatly folded, nothing more. His cash, tickets and passport must have been in his jacket pocket.

1 January, New Year's Day. The first day of the New Year wouldn't be an official bank holiday until 1974, so back then if it fell in the working week you were supposed to turn up for work. I've already told the agency I'll be off that day, so I wait all day in the bedsit – but nothing. There is no one I can ring, nothing I can do. About 4 pm, a tap on the door. It's the landlady, Marjorie, the 50-something witch who lives in the basement flat and rents out the rooms. There's a call box in the house, but it's directly outside her flat downstairs, so you never hear the phone if it rings. 'A man called Michael rang for you. He said to tell you he's gone back to Holland and he'll pick up his things next time he comes over.'

For a week or so, I'm sustained by the thought that I'll

see him, that he'll explain things, that somehow gentle, sweet, loving Michael will come back again and New Year's Eve will be forgotten. We will go back to our wonderful, loving relationship, won't we? I manage to get myself onto the Northern line from Highgate underground station each grey morning, get into town, type at my desk. I am waiting, in a holding pattern. And I continue to wait. But nothing happens. I don't know the name of the Dutch agency where he works and, even if I did, what could I say to him over the phone other than 'Come back' or 'Tell me what's wrong'. I can't do a thing.

In February, I go to Benidorm with my friend Jeanette from the shoe firm, a cheap winter sun package we'd booked ages earlier. Benidorm in winter is a revelation: sun, blue cloudless skies, not quite summer weather but still a welcome relief from the grey streets of north London or the hated morning burrow, with all the other wage slaves, into the tunnel-like entrance at Highgate. I confide in Jeanette about my lost love. She jokes it off. 'Oh, Jac, he probably realised what he was doing, getting involved with you. He's come to his senses: buy that man a drink!' And drink – and laugh – is what we do. Barbecues and cheap sangria: not quite a panacea for a broken heart, but they do help. A bit.

There's a letter waiting for me when I get back. The writing on the envelope is unfamiliar. It's from Michael's older sister, Marie, up in Scotland. He'd mentioned her to me, told me how close they were, how he loves her two little girls. It's a short letter. 'My dear Jacky. Michael gave me your address because he wants you to know that he won't be coming back to England. He's had a nervous breakdown. He had one before and we think he's getting better this time but he can't work. The doctors think he will improve, as long as he takes the medication, but it's best he stays here with me and the children for now. Michael didn't ask me to tell you this but he's told me many times how much he loves you, what a lovely girl you are and I thought you'd want to know that.'

I am floored. I've heard the phrase 'nervous breakdown' but beyond that, I don't know much about what it means. I think it involves some sort of mental illness, which is unknown territory to me and therefore quite scary. But what I don't understand is how it could suddenly strike like that, out of the blue, from nowhere. But perhaps there were many things I didn't know. We had lived in a kind of bubble of intense togetherness those few first months, hardly seeing anyone, adrift in our own little world of bed, love and brief trips to the pub. He'd been very adamant that the new job was a great idea because he said the people at work in London didn't like him. At the time, I'd thought they were just snobbish, because I knew lots of posh people worked in advertising. So I didn't read anything into it.

There was an address in neat capitals on the back of the envelope. Should I write? What could I say? I decided to try to find out more about breakdowns and mental illness. I went to the local library and found a couple of books. But they didn't enlighten me. These were books written by doctors in a very technical style which was really hard to understand, though the general idea seemed to be that treatment for mental illness involved either drugs or something called electroshock – later known as electroconvulsive therapy – which was definitely frightening. I didn't even want to think that Michael might have been treated this way. It was too harrowing to imagine. Even today, sadly, mental illness still carries a stigma because people don't quite comprehend it, though at least knowledge of the different conditions is much more developed. Back then, it was just a hugely mysterious and frightening topic and something you never heard people talking about very much.

For several weeks I put off writing a letter until finally, at winter's end, when the first tiny green buds of renewal appeared on the big ash tree outside my bedsit window, I sat down and poured my heart out to him. 'I hate to think of you being ill and unhappy but I am hoping so much it's over, you're getting better. You know I'm here if you want to get in touch, nothing has changed, I still love you,' I wrote. At least I'd done something. Yet the next day, as I trekked down Muswell Hill Road, I reached the post box – but I just couldn't bring myself to post it. More weeks passed. The letter lay there at the bottom of my shoulder bag. Then I just tore it up. Michael still loved me – and he had my address, didn't he?

This time, I didn't go down my tried and tested route to oblivion of going out all the time, trying new men and looking for more thrills, action and excitement. Instead, I'd come straight home from work, back to my room, make myself something to eat and go to bed early. Or I'd visit a girlfriend. Occasionally we'd go to see new, daring movies like *Five Easy Pieces* (Jack Nicholson at his horniest) or the fabulous spoof on the military in Vietnam, *MASH* (the first Hollywood movie to use the four-letter F-word) On weekends I'd still manage to see my mum, avoiding the Dalston flat if possible. It made me even more miserable to go there, even if Ginger wasn't around.

On one of our Saturday outings to Oxford Street, I blurt out the whole Michael story to Molly and I'm surprised at her reaction. 'He wasn't for you, Jac,' she tells me quite bluntly. 'That's why it happened the way it did. It was meant to be.'

I'd hoped for some sympathy, even reassurance that he might get better, come back. I knew she'd supported my dad in his daft trip to the Highgate flat but I didn't think she was anti-Michael in any big way. 'How do you know he wasn't for me? You only met him once and that was to check him out in case he was a murderer,' I snapped.

'Look, Jac, if he had that problem what good was he going to be for you? You wouldn't want to be stuck

with a man who was ill. And supposing it got worse?'
was her response.

I shut up. Thanks for nothing, Mum. Only down the
line did I realise she was simply being my mother, as
protective as any parent will be. She knew what it was
like to be stuck with a troubled individual. Ginger had a
different kind of problem – a love of the bottle and an
extreme kind of possessiveness – but what caring
mother wants anything less than the best for their child?
She'd accepted her fate. But why should something
similar be mine?

That summer proved to be a hot one in London. Yet I
went back to the beach at Benidorm twice: first in June
on a package deal and again in August, which proved far
too hot. I'd convinced an elderly West End travel agent
into getting me a cheap flight at a massive discount and
my friend Jeanette's Spanish boyfriend Miguel, a rep for
Clarksons Tours, found me a very cheap room for the
second trip. Jeanette stayed in relative luxury in the hotel
he worked from. My room cost something like 100
pesetas a night (at that time around 75p). Yes, it was
cheap. But that was all you could say about it. It was a
health hazard. Airless. In fact, it didn't actually have a
window. You had to leave the door open to get some air
in. We dubbed it The Dungeon.

I couldn't really sleep properly there. In the end,
wheezing and chesty from The Dungeon's damp and
humidity, I was glad to go home. Even though my sad

little bedsit – a room about 14 feet by 12 feet, with a tiny fridge and miserable, two-ring cooker – had little going for it. Yes, I had craved privacy. But back then Muswell Hill was dull suburbia: no one dropped in, like they had done in Circus Road. I'd isolated myself. Without a phone or a regular place of work, people couldn't easily contact me. Even if they rang the coin box downstairs, I wouldn't hear it ringing and Marjorie the Witch was too busy to bother with writing down messages, given her all too frequent and noisy love-ins with her incredibly young toyboys. (Coming out of the bathroom one morning, I spotted one very young-looking lad on his way out of her flat: on seeing me in my dressing gown, he went bright red and dived out the front door.)

So 1970 had started off badly and it continued that way. It was flat, uneventful, only lit up by the holiday sorties to Benidorm. By early autumn, the uninspiring temp job routine had really got to me. Boredom brings out the worst in us: I'd morphed from a wisecracking, laughing girl into a sullen, couldn't-give-a-damn person with hair bleached almost white – and still those dirty brown roots. In desperation, I found a permanent job in an Oxford Street office as a secretary in a public relations company who mainly handled the accounts of showbiz people. It sounded promising, but it wasn't much more interesting than the dull temp jobs. Bands like Status Quo, who had their first hit with 'Pictures of Matchstick Men', were clients. Mick Jagger was on the phone a couple of times. It would have been an ideal job for a music groupie – which I wasn't. I was drawn to the bright lights of showbiz glamour, but the agency was run by a couple of older men in old fashioned suits who spent much of the day away from the office and there really was nothing to do most of the time. The interesting, important and confidential work was done by an older woman who had been working with the company for years.

I started going out for longer lunches, trawling the rails of the Oxford Street stores – and coming back late. At first, no one said anything, though the somewhat frosty atmosphere in the office should have told me to stop my long lunch hours right then. After a couple more weeks, they sacked me: I'd been there just over a month. This was a huge shock. I'd never been sacked before. Years later, I heard on the grapevine that my dismissal was down to my sneery, clever-dick demeanour. It might have been tolerated elsewhere, but '50s-style employers – and despite the pop music youth explosion, showbiz back then really was run mainly by older, conservative men from the post-war era – saw no reason to put up with defiant secretaries with attitude who took the piss. Especially if the company boasted money-making big names as clients. I went back to temping the following week.

At this point, with winter looming, getting away to

sunnier, distant climes became something of a recurring idea. In fact, 1970 marked one extraordinary development, barely noticed by me at the time, but it would soon transform the way everyone travelled. That year saw the takeoff of the first commercial flight from New York to London of the Boeing 747, the jumbo jet, poised to transport people across the world on long-haul flights at affordable prices by the middle of the decade. Yet all I was doing was temping again, trudging back to my sad bedsit in my big maxi coat, my thoughts full of ideas of fleeing Muswell Hill, the uninspiring jobs and the aftermath of Michael's loss. Oh, how I wanted an escape hatch. The Dungeon experience had briefly diminished the appeal of Spanish beaches. There had to be somewhere else I could run to.

I have always had a strong opportunistic streak. Mostly, it serves you well to believe that once you spot a promising opening, you should grab it with both hands. Yet when it comes to travel, venturing out into the unknown, you sometimes need a little bit more than just the opportunity. Cash helps. So does a bit of knowledge about where you are heading, what you might expect. Research, in other words – easily achieved now at the touch of a button but slightly more difficult in the days where printed information, mostly books, was your main source of information apart from meeting other travellers. But then again, if you are headstrong, desperate to pack a bag and move on, just for the sheer hell of it, very little will stop you anyway. And so, in the autumn of 1970, I found my place to run to, a beautiful place, certainly, but one where I learned that many women didn't yet have the freedoms I now took for granted. My running away exercise didn't turn out to be a total disaster. But neither would it prove to be a raging success.

CHAPTER EIGHT

BOLO DI CREMA

I didn't realise it, but my escape plan was kick-started by a chance meeting, in the spring of 1970, at a bus stop in Tottenham Court Road. A dark-haired girl around my age, sporting a fashionable maxi skirt, wandered up to me and asked for directions. We got chatting. On the bus, conversation flowed easily: Ines was Portuguese, vivacious, interesting, living in Fulham. 'Here is my phone number if you would like to come and visit me,' she smiled as I got off at my stop.

I did visit. A new friendship was formed. Though from vastly different worlds, we discovered we had similar ideas about independence and life, and a bond was quickly established between us – the educated girl from a very comfortable middle-class home near Lisbon and the East Ender, already with a past but with very definite views about freedom and sex. Effectively, Ines was on the run. She couldn't be independent. Her family in Portugal funded her stay in London, paid the rent on her tiny flat and doled out a small monthly allowance. Yet she could not go home. She had a three-month old son, Luis, the love child of a wealthy young man from a very prominent Lisbon family. 'My family don't really want us back,' she explained that first time I visited, smoothing her black, glossy curls off her face. 'If I go back with the baby, everyone will know about us.'

At that point, I started to understand that English girls were more fortunate than their European counterparts. Not only were more relaxed attitudes towards sex and permissive behaviour slowly starting to become acceptable but the pendulum had already swung in our favour towards legal abortion and contraceptive advice for single women. Yet in other European countries, nothing much had outwardly changed for women: being open about unmarried sex remained as socially unacceptable as illegitimacy. Social attitudes in strongly Catholic countries like Ireland, Spain, France, Italy and Portugal remained as stratified and rigid as they'd ever been. Unmarried women who fell pregnant carried all the blame: they'd 'fallen' but the men weren't burdened with shame. Ines' situation was even worse than my former flatmate's. It wasn't just social attitudes or scorn: her heart had been broken too. She'd fallen madly in love with her child's father, which was why she'd thrown caution to the winds and embarked on a passionate romance with him. Now, here she was in a shabby Fulham flat with her baby son. The lover she still idolised had rejected her. Facing the wrath of his own rich, powerful family, he had recently stopped all contact. He refused to acknowledge his child. The two families were at war. An illegitimate male heir to the wealthy family's lineage was the last thing they wanted.

To me, there was something romantic and very brave about Ines' plight. After all, she'd only fallen in love and what was wrong with that? I couldn't help in any practical way, but I kept in touch, went to Fulham occasionally on Sunday afternoons, phoned for chats. Ines was a natural mother and had adapted easily to the practical demands of motherhood, balancing little Luis easily on one shoulder while warming his bottle with one other hand. Her calm courage impressed me: she seemed to be coping. Yet after a while, life got more difficult for her. Alone, she could survive in London, working part-time in a restaurant, but with a baby and unable to work at all, it was nigh impossible. 'My parents have told me they want me to come back,' she told me over the phone a few weeks later. She was close to tears. 'They want to see their grandchild. And we have servants at home, so there will be plenty of help with him. But I don't want to go.'

Yet she had to go. Luis would be better off in the comfort of her family home, no matter how bad her circumstances, how angry her family were that she'd brought shame upon them with an illegitimate child. 'If ever you want to come to Portugal, Jacky, you must let me know,' she told me on the phone before she left. 'It's really beautiful. We have a beach house in Costa de Caparica. Maybe you could come next year?'

I could. But Impatient Woman didn't want to wait till next year, too far away. Ines had often told me about Lisbon, how beautiful it was, built on seven hills, like Rome. She'd said how easy it was to jump on a train from the heart of the city to its nearby beaches, sunny resorts like Estoril, with its big casino and grand Belle Époque buildings where the rich and titled had once partied in considerable splendour. It all sounded fascinating.

So when a few weeks later, I received a long letter from her in her big, rounded scrawl, telling me how her family adored Luis but that she missed her freedom in London, I made a snap decision and immediately wrote back. Here was the answer to my restless desire to run off abroad, somewhere warm and sunny. 'I can come there now,' I wrote. 'All I have to do is give my notice on the bedsit, tell the agency I'm going away and leave all my stuff with my parents. London is driving me nuts.'

By the time Ines wrote back enthusiastically, with advice on where to stay in Lisbon, how she looked forward to seeing me, I'd bought a train ticket to Lisbon and told everyone I was off. Typically, I just dived in.

There was no period of thinking it through, asking myself all the relevant questions. My friends were mostly shocked. 'But what will you do once you're there?' (from the men), or 'I've heard Portugal is a very dangerous place' (from the women). In fact, no one I knew had actually been there. Of course, there was the small factor of the language barrier. To augment my smattering of French and Italian, I did take the trouble to buy a Portuguese phrase book, assuming it was similar to Italian or Spanish, so if I learned some phrases phonetically, I'd be fine. Talk about naïve.

Predictably, Molly and Ginger were appalled when I lugged all my belongings up the stone stairs to their flat and deposited them in my tiny childhood bedroom, still damp, still noisy from the timber yard opposite. I wouldn't stay there, even the night before I took off. The plan was to quit the bedsit in the morning and go straight to Victoria station with my suitcase that same day. Thanks to work, I had managed to scrape together what I believed was a sufficient amount of money. It'd all be fine. A real adventure at last.

Very little of my Lisbon adventure would pan out as it had formed in my over-enthusiastic imagination. I had no idea about the length of the journey, for a start. The interminable train trip took more than three days. First there was a cross-Channel ferry, then a train to Paris Gare du Nord, a metro ride to the Gare d'Austerliz and then through France for over 14 hours to the French border town of Hendaye, into Spain via Irun, across Spain for a 13-hour train ride (Burgos, Valladolid, Salamanca to the Spanish/Portuguese border at Vilar Formoso). Finally there was a switch to a Portuguese train, which was a real shock. This was ancient, dirty and a tad scary for a young English woman who had never travelled abroad alone. On the first leg, across the Channel, I had chatted to other travellers, gleaned basic info. But after we'd gone past France, my limited language skills left me without company. I didn't even attempt communication with any of my fellow passengers, mostly country people lugging huge bundles and boxes or weary, black-clad women, some carrying small children.

Food was a problem because I hadn't considered it. I just had to trust to luck – dive off the train when it stopped at a big stop and find something quickly. Fortunately, the stops were often several minutes long – and there were sometimes small stalls on the platform, selling strange but edible snacks. At least I'd bothered to change up most of my money into escudos (the Portuguese currency of the time) and I still had a few pesetas hoarded from my Spanish trips.

On the last leg, from Coimbra to Lisbon, I found myself alone in one of those old-fashioned, enclosed carriages. So unusual was it for a woman to travel alone, especially in second class, that two uniformed guards were posted to stand outside my compartment. They spoke to me in unintelligible, rapid-fire Portuguese. I tried a few English phrases, some French words. Nothing. They remained outside for the long journey, staring at me, this object of considerable curiousity, a Foreign Woman. Very unnerving. It should have warned me that attitudes to lone women were somewhat different where I was heading.

Lisbon is one of Europe's oldest and most beautiful cities. It has a magical charm that is quite unique. Europe's most southerly capital, it has stunning old buildings, narrow, cobbled streets and a romantic atmosphere. But I was not in any way prepared for the reality of arriving there, into the bustling, crowded Baixa shopping area and Rossio Square, where Ines had booked me a room in a small, noisy pension. Heat, incessant clanging trams, unfamiliar sounds and smells: essentially, total culture shock. It left me in a precarious state emotionally. My attempts to use the phrases I thought I'd learned phonetically were laughable. Portuguese is nothing like Spanish, though I did pick up that some people understood a bit of my shaky French. Troubled, I tossed and turned that night in the tiny pension bed – at least the room had a window overlooking the noisy square. What would lie ahead?

What faced me was a rather strange time. Ines wanted to help me but she was very much trapped by circumstance, living in her family's big villa on the outskirts of the city. She arrived at Rossio Square the next morning to meet me, take me back to her home, a train ride away. The atmosphere in her house – a big, turn of the century villa, surrounded by beautifully tended gardens – was so daunting, unwelcoming and cold, I couldn't wait to leave. I didn't even meet her family, though I got the impression they were in the house. Surrounded by servants – older, unsmiling female retainers in dark clothing, women who knew only repression and dutiful service and who had virtually taken charge of her baby, Ines – a lively, intelligent and attractive woman – was stranded, an object of derision, not pity, in a wealthy home where her existence was now merely tolerated. She adored Luis. So how could she leave?

'You are so free, Jacky,' she told me sadly as she accompanied me back on the short train ride back to Rossio Square. It was then that I started to understand fully what it all meant. I'd blithely assumed that the sexual revolution and emerging independence for women existed for everyone around my age – you just had to take advantage of it, make your choices and run your own show.

But of course, that was nothing like the truth.

Yet for all this, Lisbon and the coastal resorts of Estoril and Cascais were – and still are – beautiful places: leafy resorts with broad sandy beaches, tinged with a long-lost former grandeur certainly but nonetheless pleasant, even idyllic havens to while away the last months of the year. One of the wonderful attributes of Portugal for the stranger is that its people are gracious, polite and reserved. They give the stranger their space, regardless of the cultural differences. I was certainly a real oddity back then as an unaccompanied female – but I never felt particularly threatened or in danger. No one came up and started hassling me on the street. And Lisbon's winter climate is mild compared to northern Europe. I wound up sponging, living off the generosity of Ines' contacts in the English-speaking expatriate community in comfortable surroundings, far more salubrious than my shared flats in London or the Dalston grot hole, if the truth be told.

This was a relatively safe, middle-class world that I'd fallen into. They made me welcome because I was a young girl from the swinging city but also because well-travelled people in the small expat circle relished the diversion of someone from afar: the hippie traveller syndrome of young people moving around the world at will was well established now. While I was hardly a hippie, a guest from London with plenty to say, to boot, was a bit of a novelty.

Lisbon has long had an English-speaking expat population. It was nominally a free port and, as a result, a haven for spies during World War II. Portugal itself remained very much under the restraining thumb of the dictator Salazar from 1932 until 1968 and it was not until a huge revolution in 1974 that the dictatorship era ended. So life there really didn't change very much for nearly half a century, though it had always been a pleasant place for foreigners, given its beauty and Mediterranean climate. Through the friendly expat network, Ines immediately put me in touch with Alice, a blonde, smartly dressed American divorcee who cheerfully put me up for a week after my two nights in the Rossio pension.

Alice, who lived in a large apartment quite close to the Estoril area, drove me round the area, fed me, showed me how to get the train into Lisbon on the suburban line that runs from Cais do Sodre station down the coast to the resorts of Estoril and Cascais, and explained all sorts of small things I needed to know. She even had a little evening gathering to introduce me to her friends. She warned me about the men too. English girls had a rubbish reputation.

'They'll think you're easy because that's what they hear – and they can't get their hands on their own women,' Alice said. 'Be very careful what you do. If you sleep with one, they'll treat you like dirt. And they'll tell everyone, so you'll be branded a whore.'

What? Even knowing Ines' plight, I hadn't expected this sort of narrow attitude, mainly because I never considered others' motivations, being far too focused on my own desires and emotions. And I wasn't a small town girl, anyway. Suffice to say, I ignored her advice. By now, I'd long stopped taking the pill. I hated the symptoms, either blowing you up or, when trying the low-estrogen variety, Minovlar, reducing interest in sex – and had followed the advice given to me that summer at the Marie Stopes clinic in Whitfield Street, off Tottenham Court Road, to use a Dutch cap (or diaphragm to use the correct term) as a means of contraception. Using a cap was messy and it wasn't good for spontaneous love-making. But for all that the little rubber cap had, sadly, remained unused after Michael's departure, I'd popped it into my luggage, just the same. You never knew…

The Portuguese men I met in Lisbon, introduced to me via Alice's expat circle, were outwardly sophisticated, spoke excellent English, had good jobs and were well travelled. But the surface hid the truth: they were nothing like the men I'd known at home because their culture carried some very clear distinctions. Women were either sisters, mothers, fiancées, wives – or whores. Single women could flirt all they liked – that was accepted – but when it came down to it, the line was clearly drawn. If single women let go sexually, they'd be branded. Forever. Hence Ines' plight because she'd been caught out, which was even worse. Rather than sensibly accepting Alice's advice as a useful primer, of course I had to find all this out for myself. I had one brief fling, with Diego, a handsome airline captain in his thirties, a friend of Alice's English boyfriend who worked for a big multi-national.

Darkly handsome in the Latin way, with huge eyes, Diego was utterly charming, gracious and, in all truth, I couldn't wait to get into bed with him after our second romantic outing. We'd been in a pretty restaurant in Lisbon's fascinating, ancient Alfama quarter with its hilly, cobbled streets and atmospheric fado music bars. He drove me back to his bachelor apartment in a modern building in the suburbs, fondling my knee with one hand, smiling at me promisingly. This was going to be hot. I could tell. And it had been a long time between lovers. In his cool, tiled bathroom, I fiddled with the Dutch cap and readied myself for love.

I needn't have bothered. It was awful. Clumsy. Far too quick. A sexual write-off. When I thought about it later, he made even Carnaby Street Dave look quite good (and he'd been pretty rubbish). Then, just as I'd been warned, Diego's attitude changed immediately. He went into the bathroom, quickly showered, came out and coldly ordered me to get dressed *now*. He rushed me out of his place – was he scared someone might spot me? – and drove like a maniac back to Alice's apartment, 15 minutes away along the Marginal, without a single word. It was pretty obvious he couldn't wait to see the back of me.

I said nothing, closed the car door quietly behind me, though I was sorely tempted to slam it hard. Mentally, I was seething, furious with myself. Some men are better lovers than others – that is a fact of life. Some fall asleep straight afterwards. That's nature. But what I had never encountered so far was a total and very obvious loathing for my presence the minute the brief act itself was over. Was he disgusted with me, or himself? I never told Alice

I'd indulged with Diego, but she seemed to pick up on what had happened, anyway. A few days later, she told me she had another Portuguese friend, Carlos. He was single, worked in a bank in Estoril near the casino and had a large apartment in Monte Estoril, a few minutes walk from the central part of Estoril. Staying there would be better for me because it was more central than her flat which was only easily accessible with a car. Carlos had told her there was plenty of room for the English girl if she wanted to stay there.

I wound up staying in Carlos' flat for several weeks. He was short, stocky, really lively company, had travelled a lot and seemed to get what I was all about. Still a tad confused by my initial encounter with the airline man, at first I assumed he would jump on me, so I'd have to be wary. Yet he didn't. He had someone, anyway, a pretty blonde English girl who was living in Vancouver. He'd be going to see her there soon. Her photo, in a big silver frame, was prominently displayed in the living room of what was a comfortable, carefully furnished apartment with dark furniture and cool, tiled floors with a spacious, flower-decked balcony.

The problem was, with nothing much to do in the day except sleep late (until the daily servant arrived to clean) then wander down to the seafront – it was mild and sunny in the daytime, even though it was November – my routine became a permanent loll around a café, reading or taking long walks along the coastline, returning to the flat just before nightfall, then hanging around for Carlos and dinner. Quite soon, a sort of Carlos dependency developed. I already had too much time on my hands to think about Michael and to wonder what had happened to him. I wrote him many letters, but never posted one. My usual confidence, so high when I had left London, had ebbed away after the Diego incident. I was staying in a smart area, in a pretty environment. But I wanted some comfort, some reassurance that I was still a desirable woman. None came. I became quite downcast. This wasn't what I'd expected.

Carlos did whatever he did at the bank in the day. Most nights, he'd phone a friend, Marcos, a skinny sidekick who worked at Lisbon's Ritz hotel and usually the three of us would dine out, sometimes in places along the coast in Cascais, mostly in cheaper tiny local places around Estoril or Lisbon. The food was terrific: fish, rice, rabbit, liver and soups, all unfamiliar dishes but always tasty and, oh, so filling. But it was the Portuguese desserts that hooked me: the sticky, sweet cakes in the cafés and the hardy perennial, a caramel confection called a *pudim flan*, that satisfied my ongoing craving for sugar.

Soon, it became a regular afternoon ritual as I lazed away my time. I'd point to a cream cake, *bolo di crema*, and they'd hand me half a dozen small, sweet, creamy delights, so I'd stuff myself with them, all in anticipation of more stuffing of my face at dinner. There wasn't anything else to do. Sightseeing, guidebook in hand, to me, was something older people did, though I did manage to take the bus to the hill town of Sintra, a beautiful spot with the most stunning 19th-century buildings, Moorish palaces and exquisitely tended gardens.

Such was my need for reassurance, I decided I wanted Carlos. He was really good fun. He flirted outrageously with me, sometimes leaving me little notes on my bed to deliberately wind me up: 'I was here to screw the Mad English but she had gone out,' he'd scribble. Or: 'Today I went down to the beach and everyone said: "Where is the Mad English with the mad eyes?" Is she coming back?' And so on… Yet there was no way Carlos would be having his way with me. In time, I suspected he thought I was a bit of a slapper, anyway, talking endlessly about London and 'screwing', wandering off each day to walk around Monte Estoril, basically doing sweet FA. And his passion for Vancouver Girl was evident. He wanted to marry her.

So there it was, a rejection of my charms. Why did I care? I was having a free holiday, living in someone else's apartment with a servant to clean up after me, dining out at my host's expense, even getting a low level suntan by day – yet all I focused on for most of my time in Estoril was getting an amusing, yet not overwhelmingly attractive man into bed. And not quite accepting why he wouldn't come near me, even though it was blindingly apparent from my one previous experience with Diego that this was a very different culture and I'd be wise to forget about it. Some men, amazingly, were immune to my charms. How bad could it be?

Holidays are one thing, but stepping long term out of your normal environment into a totally different one, remaining totally unoccupied, just drifting along, is never a great idea. It happens all the time with people who rush off to live in sunny climes. It's just too easy to lose yourself in over-indulgence, drinking, eating far too much. Yet I drank less there than I would at home. Carlos and Marcos didn't overdo it, anyway, and it was just a glass or two of wine before or port after dinner. I couldn't afford to booze during the day. So my real Portuguese indulgence, through sheer, total boredom, became eating. My waistline expanded. Everything got tighter, though I blamed Carlos' faithful daily, the servant who took away all my dirty stuff and returned it washed and perfectly ironed. I went from shapely to chubby in a matter of weeks: she was shrinking everything. Portuguese hand-laundering was clearly not up to the same standard found in London launderettes. That was the problem.

By December, my money had dwindled to virtually nothing. I'd spend during the daytime on everything from coffees, drinks and newspapers to stamps. I penned many letters home to friends, writing back to Molly and Ginger saying I was having a great time but didn't know when I'd return. I'd already learned in the odd English paper I could buy that the country was poised for a dreadful winter of strikes. There'd already been a council worker walkout and overtime ban that autumn, with smelly rubbish piling up in the streets and troops even called out to clear the streets in some places. It was a good time to be somewhere else. Yet although though the Portuguese escudo bought quite a lot more than it would have back home, money was rapidly becoming a problem.

I asked Carlos if I could I find some sort of work but he came up with nothing. 'They don't have jobs for Mad English, Jacky, it's too risky.' Then I rang Alice, asked her to put the word around the English-speaking community. She didn't sound very confident. Yet a couple of days later, she rang back. She had something.

'You may not be interested, Jacky, but it's an artist friend of mine, Jeremy. He's lived here for years but he always has problems finding models to pose for him – er – without clothes. The local girls won't dream of it, of course. But I thought you might not mind…' Alice had clearly sussed me out. Nude modelling? Sure. Ask the Mad English. Not much money in it? Never mind. This was not my proudest moment, since I had never considered removing my clobber as a money-spinner. Until now. I fronted up at Jeremy's leafy studio near Cascais, posed for him with my wrapover printed top off while he drew furiously, silently, for about half an hour. A lean-framed, scruffy, slightly pongy English artist in his

169

fifties, Jeremy made no attempt to touch me, thankfully. And the escudos – about the equivalent of £2 – were eagerly handed over. If I liked, he said, I could come back every week. A regular job.

But afterwards, over my daily *bolo* stuffing session in my regular Monte Estoril haunt, I reflected that this was all a bit ridiculous. I'd come here for an adventure and all I was doing was getting fat, not getting laid and now posing with my tits out. An early, if plump, Page 3 girl. (Amazingly, the *Sun*'s Page 3 feature first saw the light of day that same month in 1970 – which resulted in raised voices in the Parliament and ever-increasing sales for the paper.) Perhaps what I was doing was some sort of respite from the loneliness of my dreary Muswell Hill bedsit or my life as an indifferent West End temp with a big clackety typewriter and a bad attitude. But this still wasn't exactly *la dolce vita*. I wouldn't have taken such a 'job' back home, would I?

It was inevitable, really. I dug out my return ticket, took the little train that runs from Monte Estoril station to Lisbon the very next day and went to the ticket desk at the Cais do Sodre station. After an exchange consisting of a few badly pronounced Portuguese words, a sentence or two in French, a few Italian words and even a bit of English, I had a new return date, 24 December. I'd travel over Christmas but see in 1971 on home territory. Plenty of time to work out what I'd do when I got back during the long, tedious train ride. At least I'd be prepared for the marathon journey this time, with food and water packed, thanks to my last precious escudos. Now it was my turn to ring Ines to say goodbye.

'Say "Hello" to London, Jacky,' she told me sadly. 'Maybe they'll let me come and see you one day.' Carlos had to work, so he couldn't drive me to Lisbon and wave me off. 'I will miss the Mad English,' he joked as we promised to keep in touch.

This time the long, long train ride didn't seem quite so tortuous. I'd paid a small supplement to go first class for the Portuguese section, which meant a bit more comfort and I didn't get the two miserable guards, grim-faced, outside. Christmas Day came and went as the almost empty train made its way slowly to the Spanish border and by Boxing Day I was nearly in France. My festive season lunch, stuffed into my case, consisted of spicy Portuguese sausage and bread, plus a couple of stale Portuguese cakes. Why is it that the return journey is always faster somehow, no matter how long the trip? By the time I'd reached Paris, almost two days later, and opted to walk, lugging my bag, from the Gare d'Austerlitz to the Gare du Nord for the train ride to Calais, I noted with total disgust that I could no longer do up the zip on my beloved tight, green velvet trousers from Fifth Avenue. I was just too fat.

A chubby, dishevelled size 14, my trousers held up only by a safety pin, I boarded the cross-Channel ferry at Calais on a wintry evening at the end of 1970. It was a huge relief to chat to my fellow travellers without having to worry about making myself understood in another language. Yet my prospects, whether regarding men, money or job, were zilch. My country seemed to mirror this somewhat bleak state of affairs. The newspaper headlines warned that Britain was poised for more upheaval, disputes, union walkouts and worse, though I'd just missed the dreadful power workers' work to rule that was almost as bad as an out-and-out strike. It had meant awful power cuts throughout the day and night and candles at a premium, soaring in price to 15 shillings.

It didn't sound good. Yet with my vague but omnipresent optimism, I figured I'd overcome any problems. Somehow. But the extra weight would have to come off if I were to regain my old pulling power.

CHAPTER NINE

MR VERY, VERY DANGEROUS

They conned people. They took out carefully worded advertisements in upmarket newspapers. Then they encouraged their leads (those silly enough to respond) to visit them, climb the narrow stairs to their office with the swish address – and hand over what was often their lifetime's savings. In return for their cash the hapless punters got promises – and, if they were lucky, big boxes of useless equipment. The conmen's promises of future wealth, early retirement, a life free from money woes were just words. Yet in the time-honoured tradition, the lure of the dream, the clever confidence trick, proved so much stronger than the need to stop, think and exercise caution. *Caveat emptor*, indeed.

These conmen were my bosses that short, hot summer after my return from Lisbon. It was a time of grey, suede wedge slingbacks, leather-look tiny waistcoats, suede hot pants with matching jerkins and long Indian cotton skirts. In a few months, I shed the cake weight acquired in Lisbon, though it was more a diet of white wine and not much else (glass after glass of cheap white L'Hirondelle) and snatched snacks at odd hours that brought the weight down. I'd like to recount that by then I'd become less restless, less prone to go for the instant high, the party, drink and tumble into bed with whoever I fancied. But what happened was that the party option kept winning.

There were plenty of people around me with similar ideas. Many 20-something former 'straights' were now living the hedonistic, hippie-inspired life, doing whatever they fancied – and making good 'bread' out of it. These were north London hippie types like my friend Alan, who'd ditched a safe surveyor's career because his boss wouldn't let him take his dog to the office. He swapped surveying for life as a traveller-cum-entrepreneur, driving down to Spain and Morocco with an eclectic harem of blonde sylph-like 'dames' for company, haggling for the dirt cheap cotton, silk and cheesecloth gear in Marrakesh markets and selling it to the boho locals in his tiny shop, Aurium, on Rosslyn Hill in Hampstead, next door to Lloyds Bank.

Just around the corner from the shop, Alan lived in hippie splendour in Gayton Road with an assortment of cosmopolitan dropouts, Vietnam draft dodgers, groovy Californian surfer types and young women from

Scandinavia and northern Europe. If I fancied dipping into this more alternative world on the weekend, I'd make my way there, lie on the sofa smoking with some of Alan's crazy houseguests, listening to new music like Santana's 'Oye Como Va' (from the *Abraxas* album) or 'Big Yellow Taxi' (Joni Mitchell, *Ladies of the Canyon*). This was light years away from the everyday world I mostly inhabited, working in an office in central London to support myself before roistering in the pub with all the other office wage slaves.

My nights were my own and pub life for me equalled adventure, release from the dull reality of living. I was once again living with my parents in Dalston after Portugal. I never thought I'd do this, but it was my best option. Staying there while I tried to save a bit of cash, get back on my feet, was just about manageable – but only just. I'd sacrificed a chunk of my freedom in my mad, impulsive dash to Lisbon. Once back in London, I hadn't asked anyone I knew if they could put me up for a while. Not that anyone had any room, anyway. Most people I knew lived in cramped, rented quarters. A couple of single girlfriends were boldly trying out independence in rented bedsits. They were free but it was still quite grim. These were the truly shabby years of rented accommodation on a modest salary. Others, like my friend Jeanette, remained with their parents. Or lived with new husbands in tiny rented flats. Life was actually getting leaner. Creeping inflation meant that prices had shot up along with unemployment, which was heading for the dreaded million mark by the end of 1971.

To add to the general woes, the country switched over to the new, European-style decimal currency in the February after my return. Out went the shilling, the sixpence and the half-crowns of my childhood. Goodbye, ten bob note, replaced with the 50p piece. We'd all had plenty of warning, of course, especially in the shops. But older people, like Ginger, were angry, convinced we'd been cheated out of our heritage. 'I didn't go to war for this country for us to turn into some poncy Frog place,' I'd hear him rant to Molly, overlooking the fact that his 'going to war' didn't mean true danger or hardship. He'd spent most of his leisure time in the Royal Army Pay Corps – the financial overseers of the forces – in India, putting down bets at the racetrack and had frequently been downing double scotches in the local during the earlier war years when he'd been stationed in Kent.

Yet while the early '70s were dominated by financial crises, the shocking conflict in strife-torn Northern Ireland and the ongoing power struggles with unions demanding ever increasing pay rises, my parents were like many other ordinary working people now reaching their fifties. Their lives, though previously blighted first by war and later by my dad losing his business, were comfortable enough, with secure jobs and paid holidays (a bit of a novelty for my dad, so used to self-employment for much of his life). They never ever ventured abroad, though, because Ginger flatly refused to fly. 'I've done all my travelling,' he'd say, pointing to his years of service in India. 'You can't beat a pint at the Tartar Frigate and a week at the Royal Albion,' he'd say, proudly referring to what had become their annual holiday in Broadstairs. 'Good enough for Charles Dickens, good enough for me.'

Much to my chagrin, their cramped flat, now even noisier than ever with the timber yard opposite going at full tilt, also remained 'good enough' for my parents with its cheap rent, which by now had gone up to just £3 a week. It was far too late, really, for them to take the plunge and move elsewhere, though they did venture to have a look at a widely advertised and very new development called Thamesmead, a hugely ambitious '60s social housing project in the Greenwich/Bexley area. No, they decided, it wasn't for them when they came back from viewing it. 'Too council,' said Molly, who still saw them as being a notch above the masses in the 'private' rented grot hole in Dalston. I was angry with them at the time. It was, I thought, a chance to go somewhere nicer. But I was quite ignorant and very wrong. With poor transport links, no shopping facilities and plagued by all manner of construction and social problems, Thamesmead was a dream that never fulfilled its early promise. It was just far too grandiose a plan to succeed.

These were transitional times, really. Everyone moaned constantly about the cost of everything but when you look back, things still cost very little out of most pockets, the average wage being around £40 a week. A Mars bar at lunchtime? 2p please. A loaf of bread? Dig out the new 10p piece. Even Ginger's ticket to watch his Spurs win the League Cup against Aston Villa at Wembley in February 1971 cost him just £2. Lots of things about the early '70s were quite grim, but people's lives weren't anything like as tough as they'd been while I grew up in the '50s. By the end of the '70s, nearly all my friends would be mortgaged, happily ensconced in their own homes. Even hippie Alan eventually stopped ranting against consumerism and claiming 'all property is theft' and became a bearded, kaftan-wearing homeowner with a living room disguised as a souk. But not in 1971.

For me, the key attraction of my full-time job with the conmen in offices near Oxford Street was this: they paid way above the going rate. I got £30 a week, no deductions, each Friday. No questions asked on either side. And much of our time was spent in their favourite pub, the Spread Eagle, near Bond Street. The booze flowed, frequently followed by a meal somewhere in town. Others might be a bit short of the readies but for the conmen the cash was only there to splash.

Some nights I'd return to Dalston, others I'd be 'staying with a friend'. Molly was bewildered, glad that I was there when I was but often dismayed at how rootless and unfocused I'd become. But she was busy: she'd switched back to her pre-war working environment in the West End now, with a part-time job selling wedding dresses at Berketex on Oxford Street. Ginger, now leading his nine-to-five life with the BMA, would be asleep when I did come home or up and out before me early every morning.

I slept in my childhood room, its damp walls still papered with my teenage magazine cut-outs, the early '50s black-and-white Elvis torso shots facing the leggy, high fashion '60s models with straight glossy hair and sharp, short outfits. Icons of their respective eras with torn, crumpled edges.

There weren't big rows and screaming matches with my dad as there had been in my younger years. Just a solid block of resentment in my heart for the misery, the dank perspective of those claustrophobic surroundings. And from Molly and Ginger a sort of sad, unspoken disappointment that their offspring so bright, so promising in childhood, had effectively morphed into a runaway typist without much of a future. Not even a hubby in sight. Yet I remained disinterested in husbands, my future. That night's entertainment in a glass would suffice, which is ironic when you consider how my early years were blighted by my dad's commitment to the pub.

At work there wasn't much to do for the conmen. Secretaries were hired to decorate the place, joke with, buy drinks for. Our employers were a small band of salesmen who'd grouped together around their big scam. It was what is known as a pyramid-selling venture, the general idea being convincing punters that they could make their fortune by handing over their savings to buy the goods. The idea was those who handed over their cash could then recruit others into the scheme to market the goods, who in turn would hand over their cash to the first lot and the next lot, in turn, were supposed to recruit more people, handing their money over to the second lot and so on. In this particular case, people just handed over their money and some received boxes of unmarketable and worthless fire-fighting equipment. That was it.

Pyramid schemes come and go over the years. They are usually hotly debated, some insisting even now that they can and do work. Mostly, they are rubbish. Many customers at the firm I worked for didn't even get the boxes of useless equipment to store for ever in their garage. They just lost their savings. Later in the '70s, the law would seek out such fraudsters and bring them to book. But it would be far too late for these unlucky punters.

There was only one other woman in the office and the conmen tended to treat her with considerable respect. They seemed in total awe of her. Big George (her real name was Georgina) ran the accounting side of things. (Did she too have much to answer for? I never knew.) She was a mountainous divorcee from south London with an extremely pretty face, a mane of thick, dark, curly hair, expensive clothes from Jaeger and Peter

Robinson (a now vanished department store in Oxford Street) and a formidable power over men.

Rumour had it that in his early Dartford years, Mick Jagger had bedded Georgina. Once. I believed it. She had presence and charisma. In her head, she was still the pert '60s babe who'd been chased by every bloke who met her. In reality, she was now nearly always pissed out of her brains. OK, I was well oiled a lot of the time but I was an amateur drinker compared to Big G who was often so smashed she'd be virtually speechless, reduced to the simplest of verbal expositions. 'No way! No way!' was the usual rant if she didn't like something. This would always be accompanied by much waving of arms. (Had she been studying Mick Jagger moves in her younger years?) 'Waiter! More fucking champagne *now*!' was another highlight of her repertoire, also accompanied by much movement of the upper part of her considerable body.

The call for regular infusions of expensive champagne in a bucket was also the permanent refrain of two other men closely involved in the enterprise, the brains behind the whole scheme, though they were rarely around in the office. Timothy was a short, chubby, affable, mild-mannered guy who'd gone to public school, while Adrian was a London chancer with reddish hair and pale, pasty skin, who made me laugh with his dry, sarcastic humour which matched mine. I didn't actually do any work for the bosses. My role was to type for the salesmen. But since everyone in the office was on permanent party alert we'd all wind up drinking together – nearly every night.

Adrian and Timothy also rented a houseboat on the Thames. So on weekends they'd party there and sometimes I'd join in. They were never particularly lecherous, so if any female wanted to hang out on the boat all weekend, sleep there, there was no pressure to romp with them in bed. They just wanted to party – with as many guests as possible. And they always footed the bill. This meant there was a permanent assortment of hangers on, of both sexes, as well as the hard-drinking habituees of the West End pubs, most of whom were deeply unfanciable. With the odd exception.

Nigel drank with the conmen crew regularly, lugging his briefcase up the stairs to the top bar in the Spread at day's end in his made-to-measure Hector Powe suit, eager to erase all memory of his reality – a big house in leafy suburbia and a wife and kids he hardly ever saw. Nigel claimed his business was flogging insurance – there was starting to be a lot of high pressure insurance sales at this time – but I had no idea of the truth of his circumstances. He always made a beeline for me, had a wicked sense of humour and one boozy night, before catching the 38 bus home I said yes, I'd go off with him for a dirty weekend in deepest Wiltshire. That Friday, we drove down to Wiltshire and the gorgeous 15th-century inn called the Angel in the outstandingly pretty village of Lacock.

As an assignation, it wasn't really dirty. Or even very

sexy. We were drinking pals rather than two people with the crazy hots for each other. We did make the briefest of drunken love in a low-ceilinged room in the oak-panelled inn but both of us passed out immediately after. The next day, after a huge fry-up, we spent most of the afternoon driving round, sampling the other pubs before motoring back to London. Drink-drive laws then were regularly flouted. Though the breathalyser had been introduced in 1969 and alcohol-related traffic accidents were significantly reduced after that, a lot of men like Nigel were still blasé about drinking and driving: old habits die hard.

For me, the idea that I was being driven around by a somewhat sozzled person was barely a consideration. I wouldn't dream of saying: 'I'm not getting into that car with you, you're too pissed to drive.' It just wouldn't have occurred to me. Or anyone I knew, come to that. Smoky, grubby pubs and way over the limit drivers were common then. No one ever questioned this. Apart from Molly, who would pick up my discarded clothes to wash, sniff them and say, 'They stink of booze and fags, Jac.'

I would shrug it off. 'The dry cleaners never say that, Mum,' I'd snap back.

There were many other diversions. I had many single girlfriends in north London and frequently saw Jeanette, my Spanish trip friend. She had her own drinking circle, the Kentish Town crew, wise-cracking Cockneys, down-to-earth market stall and taxi driver types, blokes who treated you with a rare East End courtliness – quite refreshing compared to the more ribald drinking scene at Conmen Central. Jeanette's friends would throw lots of parties in Malden Road council flats, young marrieds she'd had known all her life. The parties were noisy, crowded, packed with people just letting their hair down, dancing and singing along to songs like Middle of the Road's 'Chirpy Chirpy Cheep Cheep' or Dawn's 'Knock Three Times', just enjoying the release from the grind of work. Sharp-witted young Cockneys you'd find all over London back then. Now they've long moved out to Essex and beyond: the post-war working class generation that wound up living the dream their parents could never have dreamed. These days, they're home owners with holiday places in Spain, still living the good life today, born at just the right time.

The men in Jeanette's gang were hard-working lads. Only one or two were hippie, dope-smoking types with long hair, serious aficionados of the more 'intellectual' prog rock groups like Yes or King Crimson. There was definitely something appealing for me about the contrast between these glimpses of their lively, knees up, outwardly uncomplicated lives – and the dishonest, seedy personas of the champagne-quaffing, flash car driving, Bond Street conmen. Really, it was all so typical of London then, as it still remains to an extent – a jumble of very different worlds, mostly ignoring each other's existence, yet briefly rubbing shoulders – all jammed into one exciting, hectic city. A pick'n'mix social life, if you wanted it.

We weren't living in a city that was in any way as attractive as it is nowadays. If you look very closely at photos of '70s London streets, it's obvious that much of the city was still drab and shabby with signs of the immediate post-war era still very much in evidence. There were more cars, of course, but nothing like the number you see now. Much of what is now posh, super-expensive inner London was still dominated by peeling stucco and neglected, rundown, huge period houses. Bombsites were still dotted around the city. Yet the day-to-day outward drabness of their city didn't affect the Londoners' time-honoured resource: the humour, the laughter, the banter in the street markets, the shops and in the pubs. Who needed serious conversation? Everything got turned into a joke.

As for my emotional life, I'd stopped rewinding the Michael saga in my mind. A couple of months after returning from Lisbon, I'd made a trek to the house in Muswell Hill on the off chance that there was post for me. Sure enough, Marjorie the witch came to the door. Dressed up to the nines with full war paint, although it was early Saturday morning, she reluctantly made me wait on the doorstep while she tottered down to her cave.

'Only this,' she said, thrusting at me a very crumpled envelope that had clearly been opened by her and hastily resealed. Then she slammed the door in my face. It was postmarked Scotland, dated the month before. Michael's sister. She wanted me to know that Michael had left them. 'He says he's fine but I don't know where he is now,' she wrote. 'He did ring us once and said he was in Spain, looking for work. But I thought I'd let you know, in case you heard from him.'

I didn't reply. Maybe she was hoping he'd make his way back to me, but I wasn't. I never did hear from him. He vanished. There was no way of tracking him down then, unless you were really determined, and if a person wasn't formally reported missing to the authorities, that was it. In many ways, it was good to have retrieved this letter. Better to have loved and lost, I'd tell myself sometimes. Yet there were too many questions around it all for me to be convinced that what I'd felt or experienced was even the Real Thing. Perhaps it wasn't, after all. There hadn't been enough time, anyway, to really be sure.

Part of me had always held back from the significance of the 'I love you' thing, the commitment implied by a single phrase. People now constantly use the phrase 'luv ya' to finish a conversation. Which isn't a bad thing at all, openly telling people you care. We're now much more emotionally honest, or we strive to be. When I'd first hungered for independence, back in the early '60s, men often believed it was obligatory to utter those words sometimes as a sign of commitment – just to get their end away. It was like pushing a 'If all else fails, this will release the knickers' button.

By the early '70s, thankfully, we'd moved beyond that kind of emotional dishonesty because everyone was aware that having sex didn't now necessarily imply a long-term commitment. Yet I still wasn't clear about my own understanding of love or the warmth, the caring I'd felt for Michael. Passion, I knew, could be overwhelming, blind you. And the emotions engendered by really passionate sex, closeness and intimacy could sweep you up in their wake. But love itself? Clear as mud.

Yet while my mind would ponder these questions over and over again, I was now about to encounter something quite different, an emotional state that might disguise itself as intense love of a certain kind, when in reality it was far darker. And potentially damaging. Obsession. A total fixation with one person to the extent that everything in the rest of your life runs secondary, living only for the times when you're with that person. I hadn't experienced it to any extent before. I didn't understand it then. I still don't. Perhaps it's something that can happen if there's a real void in your life and I was by then vulnerable to this, because I was floundering without any focus. But this is how it happened…

I am descending the pub stairs to the street. I've left my glass of wine upstairs in the top bar of the Spread and it's so hot, I am desperate for some fresh air. But I never make it outside. Because he's there, standing at the bar, nursing a beer. I am immediately, instantly enslaved by this brooding, handsome individual. Tall, broad shouldered, darkish, shoulder-length hair, wine-coloured velvet suit, large-collared shirt, no tie. Beautiful, long-lashed green eyes. Rock star good looks but not young, about 30. Mr Darcy, go home, your time is up. Elvis, you're so over. This guy is the real deal, the works. The aura is 'I'm dangerous – but you can't resist me, anyway.' Is he English? Foreign? Is he for real, for Christ's sake? I have never seen such a sexy, gorgeous man before. I do not even hesitate, consider any propriety, deploy any game or tricks. I just walk over and start talking to him. I have to have this stranger. That is exactly what runs through my head at this moment.

As soon as I start talking, his sexy half-smile tells me he knows exactly where I'm at. Of course he does. You can tell he has a string of women, right across the city, all panting for his services: I am poised to become the newest, latest diversion. Yet that balmy June night turns into something so extraordinary to me, so unusual, so unsettling it will send me into a spiral of prolonged confusion and unruly behaviour for many months.

I'm almost right about the foreign bit. He's a half-French journalist, though he's never lived there. His mother came to England to marry a doctor she'd met in France in the 1930s. His dad died young. His mother hoped her son too would study medicine, but he dropped out of medical school after six months. He really wanted to act: he certainly had the looks and the presence, but it didn't happen. To placate his mother, he took a job on a local paper in the north and turned out to have what it took to be a trainee reporter. Now he works as a 'casual' (an early word for freelance) for a number of different Fleet Street newspapers. His real name is François, but everyone knows him as Frank.

Once we're back in his tiny, untidy, postage-stamp-size place in Belsize Park, Frank doesn't touch me. He pours us drinks and talks, asks me about myself, what I'm doing, where I come from. Then he tells me his own truth. 'I'm not the faithful type, sunshine,' he says in his silky, well-modulated voice. 'I just love women.'

Fine, I think, staring at him, longing to see what's underneath the velvet suit. I can cope with that 'loving all women' stuff. (No I can't – talk about denial.) Then he delivers the coup de grace. A fiancée called Annette. 'She was a model, now she's making good money as a croupier. I keep this flat on for the other girls. She knows what I'm like. But she's a bit naughty herself sometimes, which is probably why we get along.'

Do I head for the door? Hardly. I can't even move, so entranced am I by everything about this man: his looks, his voice, his stance. Here is a self-avowed Really Bad Boy. No lying, no pretending – things have certainly moved on in the sexual honesty stakes since the days of Jeff. Frank is throwing me the gauntlet. Not just a lover with loads of women but a Special Woman to boot. Yet he knows full well he's got me. Later he tells me that it's always my facial expression that gives my game away. And that, he says, is very endearing.

Think of love games. Consider role reversal scenarios. Think about the power of a sexy voice using exactly the right words at the right time. I won't give any more detail: suffice to say that until this point I'd considered myself sexually experienced. Really, I knew little. Until this night, a night of love like no other. After that first night with Frank, the kind of lover for whom the dawn means the briefest times of snatched sleep, I am beyond sated. My body is enslaved by him. But Frank is also accomplished, talented in love way beyond the mere physical. He reaches inside my brain, takes me to unknown places in my head. I am totally hooked. He is a powerful and potent drug. The kind of drug that some people should never take – even once.

From that point on, my obsession with being in bed with Frank rules my every waking moment. What makes it even worse is that he's a constantly moving target. He travels abroad for work sometimes. He works late. He's never ever in the same place for long. He encourages me to call him at whichever paper he's working on – 'Does it matter who calls who?' – and he's wryly amused by my very obvious, slavish dedication to our affair. He isn't just calling the shots, he owns the gun. You could call me a love junkie. But it wasn't love. It wasn't sheer lust either. It was simply a physical and mental obsession, a treacherous place to be for a woman who secretly yearned for independence and real freedom. I was trapped.

I go to the office, do the minimum of work, drink heavily virtually every night, try sleeping with other men (to disastrous effect) and live dangerously. I focus intently on my single-minded goal: working my way towards the next time I'm in his bed. For a while that summer, some sort of pattern emerges. We go to see movies like *Vanishing Point* or *Sunday Bloody Sunday* (not a great choice to watch with Frank next to me, his hand on my thigh, since the topic is a Londoners' love triangle: a gay doctor and a divorced career woman, both in love with the same young, handsome, bisexual man). *Sunday Bloody Sunday* was, in many ways, a movie that reflected the huge changes in what was becoming a much more permissive society: the sight of two men kissing would not have even reached the cinema screen even a few years before.

At one point we make up a foursome with a very good-looking friend of mine from Dalston, Deborah, and another journalist friend of Frank. 'He didn't like her, Jacky,' Frank said afterwards. 'He said her eyes were dead – and he's right.'

He's lazy, can't be bothered to pick me up or observe any of the normal conventions. He gets me to meet him in Fleet Street or West End pubs. One day he asks me to meet him at one of the newspaper offices he works in. In suede hotpants, I perch in the reception area of the big newspaper building near the Thames, drinking it all in, amazed at how dilapidated and downbeat it all looks, particularly the scruffy-looking men who rush through the lobby, clutching their notebooks, leering openly at my outfit as if they've never seen such gear before. The papers are full of photos of leggy women in hotpants: don't they read their own publications? I've never been anywhere near a newspaper office until now. I'd imagined them to be gleaming palaces of modernity, like the chrome and leather sofa posh ad agencies I'd temped in briefly. The glamour of the Street of Dreams looked, close up, like Scruffsville.

I never know when he's going to be around. One Sunday afternoon, I'm at home in Dalston when he rings from Rome and demands I come out to Heathrow and meet him off the plane. 'Can you make it, sunshine?' he entreats. 'Be great to see your smiling face.' Several forms of transport, including a cab, later (there was no direct tube or rail line to Heathrow back then; it was a real trek from Dalston) I reach the arrivals hall. He emerges silent, dishevelled and very, very smashed. In the taxi back to his flat, he passes out briefly, then tumbles straight into bed, snoring, when we arrive. I lie there, next to him, not daring to speak. I'm with him. Nothing else matters.

He is a habitual and heavy drinker. There is always a bottle of something, usually beer, by his bed. His place is a tip, even by usual male standards, but then he doesn't really live there. It's just a place to screw. Sometimes he drops me off in the morning, telling me he's en route to the west London flat belonging to Croupier Girl. I tell myself no one has him. But I am very wrong. Obsession equals a permanent state of delusion.

At the end of the summer, I buy a £30 return flight to Ibiza, my first holiday to what is then known as the hippie island and book into a cheap pension in Santa Eulalia. More endless drinking followed by getting into arguments and wine-chucking incidents. Temper tantrums leading to tables overturned in nightclubs. I'm so stroppy, so out of control, it's a miracle I survive without someone thumping me. Or worse. But I emerge intact. I head straight for a coin box when I get off the plane. Yes, he's leaving the office, will be at the flat. He's amused, mocking, when I carry my case through his door. 'You look good, sunshine. You've lost a bit of weight. But you're not as thin as you think you are.'

The very next day I discover my job is gone. While I've been away, the beautiful Deborah, she of the dead eyes, has nicked my job. They don't need me any more. This is totally my own fault. I'd told Deborah what an easy gig it was, working for the conmen and I suggested she temp there in my absence. The conmen had then taken her to the pub, decided she was prettier – dead eyes or not – and that it was easier to get her to actually do some work, since my obsession with Frank and daily phone calls to him had become a bit of an office joke.

'What did you expect, sunshine?' is Frank's only

comment when I ring with my news. 'You knew they were a nasty bunch.'

Luckily, the temp agency say they have an instant booking for me. 'They need a temp but it's a permanent job if you want it,' the agency woman tells me, handing me the card with the details, eyeing me suspiciously. 'I'm not sure if it's your kind of thing.'

It doesn't matter. One thing is already clear to me. I can't afford to be out of work and I need to be in an office during the daytime, rather than sitting around in Dalston obsessing over Frank. At least, at work, I'm momentarily distracted and it fills the daylight hours.

The temp job is in Tower House, Southampton Street, off the Strand. A publishing company called IPC. The job is profoundly dull. Two thin, grey, older men, executives in the planning department, are my bosses. A brand new IPC building, housing all the company's magazines and called King's Reach Tower, is being built near Waterloo Bridge. Another high rise, though hopefully not another Ronan Point. The men's job is to help plan the construction of the new building. This means lots of boring architects' drawings, nothing remotely interesting. 'The job's yours if you want it,' the agency woman tells me when I go to pick up my money after a very dreary week in Tower House. 'They like you and they're fed up with temps who can't spell properly. And the money's quite good, £22 a week with LVs. Provided you don't mind joining the clerical workers' union.'

Union? What union? Had I followed the political events governing all our lives rather than reading women's magazines or spending my life in the pub, I'd have understood a bit more about unions – and why the more militant ones and their demands were making life nigh impossible for many people all over the country. Strikes. Stoppages. More power cuts. At that point, there were over 300 trade unions and almost half the country's work force of 23 million belonged to one. But all Miss Opportunist thinks is: where's the scam? There had to be a benefit to joining a union, didn't there? 'I can join, that's OK,' I tell her. 'But what does it mean? Do you get any extra money, overtime or that sort of thing?'

'No. But if you join, it gives you the right to apply for other jobs in the publishing industry,' the woman says encouragingly, keen to get me to take the dull job so she can get her commission. 'Some of the jobs are really interesting – editorial jobs on magazines and papers that you never see advertised because the unions say they have to be advertised internally. All the really good editorial jobs go to people in the union. A few of the jobs do pay overtime. Most girls in those jobs stay in them for years.'

She's got my attention. The word 'editorial' has resonance for me. One big consequence of my obsession with Frank is a total fascination with what seems like an amazingly glamorous, interesting job: the world of newspapers and journalism, being a reporter. He doesn't talk about it much. But when he does, there's genuine passion in his voice. 'It's all about getting the story, sweetheart. You have to get the story. If you don't, you don't survive.' Frank's job takes him everywhere around town and off on planes sometimes. To me, restless and hungry for adventure, it seems like a charmed existence. I figure that if taking the boring job means there's even a chance of working in this exciting newspaper world out there, I'll do it.

I start at Tower House straight away. I learn that once I join the union, there's a six-month period before I can apply for any of the internally advertised editorial jobs, usually posted up by the side of the ancient, clanky lift in Tower House. I'll just have to wait. Me and my fixation with the green-eyed, long-haired man with the gorgeous voice would have to exercise a bit of patience.

With regular money coming in once more, I can leave Hackney again. I find a bedsit in Garden Road, off Abbey Road, and move myself in there at the end of that autumn, after an outrageously boozy trip with Jeanette to a place called Mojacar, all whitewashed buildings, crazy, rich American expats and bars run by dodgy, drug-smuggling blokes. They're even shooting Hollywood westerns in the arid, dusty area around Almeria. I have a steamy one-nighter with an English barman, an ex-con who is superbly knowledgeable in bed: a one-man orgasmatron. It's a flash of distraction from my all-singing, all-dancing Obsession. Have pity for the obsessed who cannot face up to the truth. Because one day, the truth will come up and hit them in the face – and they will not be able to deal with it.

One day in November, I get through to Frank at work. OK, he'll come round, see my new place. I rush home, tidy up, hopeful. Maybe he'll stay the night. 'Are you sure you want to live here, sweetheart?' he says dismissively, looking round the room which, while larger than the Muswell Hill bedsit, is just as depressing – and even more expensive at £7 a week. And no, he doesn't want to linger. He wants a drink.

It's truth time. In the Clifton pub in St John's Wood, he delivers his final bullet. Straight. 'It's Annette. She's had enough of the way we're living. And I have too. So we're getting married. After Christmas. We want to make a go of it. I feel like I've known her all my life,' he says, looking briefly at my face, then gulping his beer down in one swift movement.

I lose the plot, of course. He has never, ever lied. It's me who couldn't ever face the truth because I was always far too obsessed with getting to see him, be in his bed, to actually be able to stand back, view it all with a cool eye. I'm a '70s version of a stupid stalker, living in a daft world of my own making, living only for the next time. Yet even then, I refuse to acknowledge what is real. 'What do you mean? What, you won't see me any more? Why? Why? I don't believe you're getting married! You're just saying that to put me off!' I yell at him. Then I burst into tears and make a headlong dive for the ladies. This can't be happening. It can't! I sit on the loo, sobbing my heart out.

When I emerge five minutes later, he's gone. The car's gone too. I totter back down Clifton Hill to the bedsit and cry most of the night. The next morning, I call in sick at work. I try ringing him the next day. The guys at work have been primed: 'No, Frank's out on a job.' 'No, he's not coming in this week.' 'Frank? Are you sure you've got the right number, love?' Then, unexpectedly, after I've called for the sixth or seventh time in a week, he picks up the phone.

'Oh, sunshine. Meet me in the Kings and Keys,' he sighs wearily. 'I'll get out around eight.'

I dress up to the nines, tight black velvet jeans, new Jeff Banks flowered blouse, my hopes high. Hopes of what? you might ask. A reprieve from my prison of obsession? A night with him – and then back to more obsessing, more phone calls until I get him? I wait. At 8.30 he strides into the pub. His face is like thunder. He's sober too. His easygoing mood, a few hours back, has gone. 'Come on,' he says, yanking my arm. 'We can't talk here.'

Silently, we walk to his little MG, parked in a side street. I have no idea what is going to happen. It's like a death walk. 'Get in,' he orders and settles at the wheel as I clamber in. But we're going nowhere. He wants to read me the riot act away from the ears of his nosy colleagues. 'If you don't stop hounding me, you're in *real trouble*, sunshine,' he says, slowly and very deliberately. Frank's good at menace. I know he means every word. But pathetically, I still try.

'Why?' I bleat. Why can't we see each other? I know you're not going to marry *her*!'

'I've told you the truth to your face and you still don't get it, do you? I'm a mug. I should've done it over the phone and saved myself the hassle. It's *over* – can't you get that into your stupid head, for fuck's sake!'

I'm silent. Maybe if I shut up he'll change his mind?

He looks at me, winces visibly – and leans across me to open the car door. Wide. His voice is low. But the menace remains. 'Now get out. Go home. Don't even *think* about ringing me any more. I swear, if you make any more phone calls, I'll call your parents, tell them how you're hounding me, calling me at the office all the time. We're both sick of it, me and Annette.'

That's a swift and very painful bullet. But it does the trick: the mention of her name, the shock of discovering he's discussed my existence with her, let alone his threat to call up my parents, brings me to heel. I'm tearful now, out of his car, standing there in the narrow street, watching him drive off, back to his life with his fiancée, the life I've pretended to myself doesn't really exist.

Today I could continue to stalk him, through social networks, text messages, internet trolling – all the means of communication we deploy now that allow the deluded or angry obsessive to hoard scraps of information about the pursued and to continue stalking their object of desire. Or hatred. But then, it wasn't that easy: all I had was the phone – or the Annette flat in west London. Fortunately, I had no idea where that was. I could, of course, try his little flat at night – but that could prove either useless or even worse, if his car was outside and he was entertaining.

An obsession such as this cannot end quickly. Especially one so heavily weighted towards sex. For more than a fortnight, I stay in the bedsit, calling in sick at work, sleeping much of the time, just about managing to wander out to the shops for food, my hair unkempt, all interest in my appearance gone. Yet I do stop calling him, now that the pointlessness of it all has finally sunk in. My obsession with Frank fades away, in my mind, by increments. But it's a very slow process. In time, it will be nudged out by circumstance, other events, new vistas. Yet it continues to haunt me for a long time, though I don't try to contact him again.

The following year he marries. Some years after, they divorce and many years later, his own life in freefall, mine on an incline, we meet up, without a trace of any rancour on either side. Too much water under the bridge. But at that point in the bedsit, as I struggle with my feelings, wondering what drove me down such a crazy, intense path, I am unable to understand that knowing Frank has unwittingly nudged me towards a specific destination. An idea about working in a different kind of place that will, in time, change everything for me. For good.

CHAPTER TEN

THE CLOSED SHOP

The customs man at Gatwick is rifling through my suitcase. He looks bored. Maybe he's thinking about his lunch break. We both know what he's looking for. But I am one hundred per cent untroubled, completely guilt-free. On the other hand, my new friend Robert, with whom I've just spent an incredibly stoned few days in Santa Eulalia, has left me to my own devices as soon as we disembark from the plane carrying us from Ibiza. And I know why, though he's not told me anything. Robert, a scrawny, dark-haired 'straight freak' (his Danish hippie friend's description), a north London lad, recently married into an aristocratic family, is carrying something the customs man would love to find. Dressed for success, suit, tie, briefcase, Robert has already ambled straight through towards the exit. No one steps forward to stop him.

I grin broadly at the customs man, who knows I'm having a laugh at his expense. After all, he gets it all day, every day from returning Brit holidaymakers, tanned and impossibly pleased with themselves after their bargain jaunt to the Med.

'See? Nothing but a load of dirty knickers,' I quip, unable to resist the joke. Customs man ignores this, closes my case and stares back at me, taking in my mop of wild, brown curly hair, ankle-length turquoise wrapover cheesecloth dress, navy espadrilles and straw Ibiza basket looped over one shoulder.

'Do you know where you're goin', love?' he croaks.

'Of course. I live here!' I say brightly, picking up the case and heading out, secretly delighted that he's mistaken me for some sort of wild, untamed hippie.

It's 1974. I may have just had my third holiday that year on the hippie island and while there indulged in the traditional hippie ritual, getting stoned out of my mind on hash cookies. But I'm no dropout. Oh, no. My home is a shared flat in St John's Wood (again) and I have a decent, well paid job. I've been there for two years now and have every intention of staying there. Stability, of a sort, has entered my life as a news desk secretary on a Fleet Street Sunday newspaper. Six weeks holiday a year and £40 a week, plus occasional overtime, gives me ample freedom to indulge my fantasy life as a wild hippie woman on a Mediterranean island, reading Camus (*A Happy Death*) on the deserted beach on the tiny island of

Formentera and downing *carajillo* (coffee with brandy or rum) for breakfast, price 50 pesetas. In my own way, I am enjoying the Great British mid-'70s dream of so many ordinary people: the two-week sunshine jaunt to Spain has now become a status symbol, a must-have for the working person. Doing this twice, three times a year if I choose, is no longer a luxury. It's a right.

Fleet Street newspapers, at that point in time, were enmeshed in worker's rights. Decades later, after I'd left, I hailed a taxi that turned out to be driven by a chatty former newspaper printer. It turned out he'd been working in Fleet Street around the same time as me. Permit me to sum up 1970s Fleet Street life in his words. 'Let's face it, luv – the editors were all pissed, the printers were all pissed, the reporters were pissed – *everyone* was pissed. I dunno how they ever got the papers out, to tell ya the truth.'

He was right. Nearly everyone around me in the newspaper world at this time was very thirsty indeed. A bottle of mineral water with lunch? Unheard of. Indeed, the 'lunch hour' was a flexible concept for many working in industries like newspapers and advertising, where entertaining and expense accounts ruled. Lunch was frequently a serious business, taking three or four hours out of the day, with an equivalent number of bottles of wine – or more – on the bill. There were no smartphones or gizmos to summon people back to the office or demand an instant response – only the pub landlord's black Bakelite phone to yank the reluctant drinker back to the desk.

The hallmark of life on the news desk was the office camaraderie common to all news environments. Journalists feed off communication, challenge, gossip, repartee – and wit. It's their stock in trade. Humour above all else, in all situations. Backed up, of course, by the endless yarns in the pub about who did what last night: the right job for a girl who loved partying, men, laughter and gossip.

As for getting the papers out, thanks to workers' rights there were many times when the Fleet Street national newspapers didn't even reach the British breakfast table at all. One paper didn't appear for a whole year because of a union dispute. The union stoppages and strikes were not directly related to the drinking culture: they mirrored what was going on in many other industries across the country. Because the entire newspaper printing enterprise was then run not just by its often frustrated management but on the whim of militant and powerful trade unions in a manner that seems quite astonishing now.

Though walkouts and stoppages in all sorts of industries, often because of pay disputes, became part of Britain's history in the early 1970s, it's often overlooked that trade union militancy had featured in British life since the 1950s. But these later disputes affected so much. No post. No trains. No fuel. Dock strikes. Council workers strikes. Millions upon millions of pounds down the drain because of lost working days and productivity. And the newspaper business was caught up in all this: for many years it was accepted that the print unions ran certain Spanish practices (a very old phrase used to describe restrictive working practices, negotiated between the union and employers, yet very much in favour of the union employee).

One well-known 'Spanish practice' enabled Fleet Street printers to merely sign on for a night's shift work (Mickey Mouse was a popular name used) then either go back home or down the pub. Money for nothing. Two paypackets. Week in, week out. A gravy train and far too cushy a way of life for any of the passengers to actually want to jump off. This all ended, of course, in the 1980s with Rupert Murdoch and the big Wapping dispute when thousands of print workers lost their jobs overnight. But until that time, newspapers remained very much a union-dominated enterprise. Their managements had no choice. Being hired in the first place was complex because everyone, whatever their role, needed membership of the relevant trade union before they could be employed. The closed shop policy was eventually outlawed in 1989, but until then it was equally difficult for union members to be sacked or dismissed by management once they were in. It was all down to the union might.

I'd been drawn into the idea of working on a Fleet

Street paper because of my crazy obsession with a bad boy hack and his hard-drinking, access-all-areas lifestyle. I'd figured it was a fast-moving, stimulating sort of place where you'd have plenty of laughs (I was right about the laughs) and the idea of working at the beating heart of a national newspaper seemed vaguely glamorous. I was mistaken about the glamour.

To our eyes in the 21st century, the Fleet Street editorial office of the 1970s, where all the stories fit to print were generated, would look merely... drab. Shabby, scruffy, smoke-filled, strip-lit, vast, open-plan spaces with special areas for enormous newspaper files with wooden spines and handles. Huge metal desks with big spikes (a contraption for spearing unwanted copy). Battered old typewriters and ancient office equipment from the 1920s such the Banda (a primitive document duplicator) and the Lamson Paragon overhead pneumatic tube system, which carried paperwork and documents across the office. Elsewhere in the business world, office technology like photocopying machines already existed. But not here.

Even the reporters out on the road, phoning in urgent stories to their respective editorial teams, had to use an antiquarian, somewhat wasteful system. All their copy had to be dictated, word for word, comma for comma, down the line to telephone copy takers, seated in their own sectioned-off cubicles on the fringes of the newsroom. The copy takers would then type up the text and have it forwarded to the editorial sections around the building. I never got a chance to watch the all-important printing process itself, which took place in the bowels of the building. This was strictly off limits to the unauthorised, whatever their rank (more union rules). The demarcation lines of each and every job could not be crossed. Ever.

This was a mostly male domain, run by a fairly conservative group of editors and editorial managers, men in their forties and fifties. Their archaic world within a world carried its own unique characteristics (mostly thanks to the union rules) and, in the case of the paper I'd joined, there was an all-pervasive, powerful emphasis on maintaining the status quo. Once ensconced in a full-time staff job on a national newspaper, the editors, sub editors, reporters, feature writers and photographers had won their own comfortable berth on the gravy train. This included very generous expenses, reported to be the best in Fleet Street.

Journalists on staff could easily bank their salaries (which were also good) and live off the expenses (which tended to be part fiction, part truth) by writing 'Ent. special contact: £20.' And so on. On the *Sunday Mirror*, where I worked, the journalists' union had negotiated a four-day week: hardly a rigorous working schedule for a paper that only really got going on a Thursday.

Yet this strange world, which initially seemed so odd to me after years of chopping and changing office environments, went on to hold an ongoing, profound attraction. Not because the office routine of taking dictation, typing letters or making coffee was any different – other than that you were typing lists of freelance payments, memos or story schedules for editorial conferences – but because the newspaper atmosphere oozed a very distinctive kind of professionalism and dedication to craft. Despite the unions, the boozing in the pubs and the scruffiness, there was also much pride in the paper's success, a job extremely well done. Gravy train or otherwise, most of the editors, journalists, sub editors and photographers there had worked diligently to get onto a national newspaper. In journalism terms, once on the big Fleet Street national, they'd made it. Hence their very obvious pride in their craft.

The paper sold many millions. The company coffers were chokka with vast sums from their advertising revenues. Its readers, should they opt to turn up in reception, ring or write in, were always, without exception, treated with the utmost courtesy, even if they were nutters. (The nutters tended to write, usually on lined paper, in capital letters underlined in bright red ink with certain rude words cut out and pasted onto the letter from their newspaper of choice – and these were the more pleasant loonies.)

A news desk secretary was parked in front of a dark green metal console with half a dozen buttons linking up to the main switchboard, which would direct calls through to the desk as they came in. The job was primarily to use the phone, juggling or directing calls to the news editor or the reporters, passing on information from reporters out and about on stories – a central hub, if you like, of a vast inky enterprise. Secretaries on the paper, although their roles were mostly quite menial by today's standards (editor's secretaries got the confidential stuff, but they tended to keep themselves to themselves), were very much part of the general lively, jokey camaraderie – yet as females, we were also treated with an old-world courtesy, which came as something of a surprise.

What we'd now call sexual harassment – personal comments on your appearance, mostly – was part and parcel of working life in all offices in my twenties. You just dealt with it, no big deal. Sometimes it was fine: show me a woman who doesn't welcome the attention of a compliment? As I've said, if you didn't like it, you could deploy a sharp, cutting comment to stop it all in its tracks. If you moved offices as much as I did, you got used to the variations in attitude: secretaries in the 1970s were still either more or less ignored or treated primarily as objects of desire.

Even the advertisements that companies used to attract young women were worded in a way we'd find laughable, if unacceptable, now. Here's a typical one: 'A dolly required to brighten our lives. Must be gorgeous (or attractive will do), discreet, forgiving, with excellent shorthand typing skills. Salary? Well, ask us as much as you feel you're worth.' Today's HR bosses would have a fit, wouldn't they?

By the time I started at the newspaper in the summer of 1972, however, the moral climate had already started to shift and the feminist voice, questioning women's identity and men's behaviour, was already making itself heard, following the publication of Germaine Greer's sensational book *The Female Eunuch* in 1971. Yet it wasn't a strident war cry: the politically correct world – and the truly multi-cultural or diverse society – were still decades away.

People frequently hark back to the blatant sexism of the old, traditional newspaper world and of course it was what we'd regard now as a sexist environment – with a lot of effing and blinding thrown in. There were just two female journalists in the section I worked in – Viv, a much older woman (rumour had it she'd won the job as a result of a long-term affair with a long deceased executive) and June – a very bright, sassy younger woman, definitely going places. Yet somehow, in this place, the 'I'm well aware you're a woman' attitude was a bit more sophisticated than I'd been used to: sexism dressed up with humour. And a veneer of respect.

The sense of being part of an important enterprise was also very obvious to me. I was a cog, certainly, just one in a big wheel, but one whose role required a professional approach and a certain amount of maturity. I couldn't have appreciated this environment in my early twenties. I'd never run across any feeling of belonging in a job before or taken anything like a sense of pride in my work. Yet here, where the unspoken emphasis was on working as a team, I did. Moreover, the office hours were unusual: Mondays off, work on Saturdays, amble into the deserted newsroom at 10 am, a welcome start for anyone with a late night reveller's habit. It all added up to something quite different, though it took a while to get used to my new environment.

I'd paid my dues, in a sense, to get there. Out of economic necessity I'd again moved back to Dalston, planning to save up until I could afford another flat share. Through that miserable winter and spring of 1972 when the miners went on all-out strike for more money and power cuts became a feature of everyday life, I'd done my own time at the coal face: turning up at Tower House for the dull job, slowly recovering my equilibrium after the Frank fiasco, already scanning the lists of newspaper editorial vacancies posted by my union, NATSOPA (National Society of Operative Printers, Graphical and Media Personnel), long before I'd even completed my obligatory, slow-moving six months. But once I was through that and I spotted the *Sunday Mirror* job description, I knew it was for me.

I got the job quite easily. The news editor, Monty, was incredibly cheerful, genial and happy to hire me at my interview. Yet for some reason there'd been no mention of the fact that I'd be part of a double act, working with a more senior girl, Jenny, who'd been on the paper for many years. Fleet Street over-manning practices (in this case meaning two people doing one person's job) meant that the news desk merited two secretaries – just in case.

Jenny was on holiday on my first day in the newsroom. Everyone was polite and welcoming as I settled behind my big typewriter. But I was quite worried when I learned I'd be one of a pair. I often made friends at work: sometimes these turned into established friendships. But I knew that the dynamic between two women working opposite each other every day in what I believed was a lively environment was one that had to work: if she's a right bitch, I thought, it's going to be hell. I needn't have worried.

Enter Jenny, a very pretty, slender, long-haired girl around my age, trendily attired in a cheesecloth skirt, espadrilles and pretty stripy top, showing off her suntan that first morning back from holiday. Everyone welcomed her back, made a huge fuss of her: it was clear she was a much-loved institution. Her boyfriend, Roy, a northerner, worked on the art desk on the other side of the huge, open-plan office. Fair-haired and slim, he was also super-trendy with tiny John Lennon style rimless glasses – indeed, the pair were dubbed John and Yoko around the office. And it was true: the similarity was striking, given Jenny's long hair, very high cheekbones and slight build.

We circled each other warily for the first few days. I soon gleaned that one girl who'd worked in my new job had been a great beauty who sulked a lot. Phew. I was neither a beauty or a sulker. After a few days our initial wariness turned to laughter. You couldn't help it. Monty and Jenny shared a sharp, cutting wit. You could tell from Jenny's jokey exchanges with everyone in the place that this witty repartee was part and parcel of the news desk environment. So what was effectively a job share for two full-time employees would work: I could watch Jenny and learn too.

Apart from Jenny, there were three other people on the news desk: Monty, his deputy George and a much older man called Brian. Monty was something of a joker, but underneath his laugh-a-minute personality was a highly talented journalist. He'd been one of the youngest men ever to run a big Fleet Street news desk. Sports mad and outspoken, Monty tended to tell it like it was. Which is why the impressionable new girl on the desk never ever quite forgot Monty's war cry when he read a piece of reporter's copy that wasn't up to scratch: 'Who wrote this fucking intro? Fucking Noddy?!'

The hapless reporter would scurry up to the desk from the far end of the newsroom, duly abashed and shamed before his peers. 'Sorry, Mont, sorry…' A few hours later, Monty would be down the pub, buying the reporter beers, laughing and joshing with him. I'd heard that news editors were mostly grumpy people, too harassed and worn down by the rigours of the job to bother with pleasantries. Monty definitely confounded the stereotype.

As for George and Brian, effectively Monty's back-up team, George was a fairly low-key, modest Scottish man, his quiet manner deceptive: terrier-like when nosing out a story, his persistence was legendary. Brian was somewhat patrician, a silver-haired elder statesman of the newsroom with a plummy, educated accent and a shrewd way of sizing things up. Brian had seen it all and done it all. He'd even given up drinking many years before – which made him quite unique and a great leader of the boozy troops (the reporters). 'I'm going to be happy, chummy,' was Brian's mantra if there was an editorial crisis or a union dispute with an unclear outcome. Everyone was 'chummy'.

Exactly how the unions maintained their stranglehold on the proceedings was demonstrated to me just a week or so after I'd joined. Jenny and I were having a chat about a document that Monty needed to take into conference. The problem was, it was in an office several floors down. 'Oh, I'll just get a messenger to bring it up,' I said airily, already having noticed the two older men seated at desks near the Lamson Paragon overhead tracks and its chute which transported copy and general paperwork to the editorial floor from elsewhere in the building. I'd seen them bringing things to people's desks. So they were messengers, weren't they?

Never assume. A few minutes later, I looked up from rolling a letterhead into my clunky Remington to see a deputation of three men standing by my desk. They were all union representatives, dark three-piece suits, starched collar and tie, full of their own importance. What followed came straight out of *I'm All Right, Jack*, the late 1950s' movie where Peter Sellers plays a left-wing union shop steward in a satire about workers and unions.

'I have come to tell you that you have been overheard describing one of our union members as a messenger,' said the oldest one, a man called Tommy who had worked on the paper since the death of the old King, perhaps even before. 'Unless you cease using this kind of term to describe a union member who is called a tape room assistant, we will have no choice but to take serious action.' Then they all walked away. It's amazing they didn't click their heels, so militaristic was their body language.

Unwittingly, in conversing with my colleague, I had breached union regulations. Later, in the ladies, Jenny explained it all to me: 'You can't upset them, they've all been here for years and if you'd argued back it would have got worse. They could walk out over something like that.'

Walk out? Go where? What was this all about? This wasn't *The Rag Trade*, was it? (*The Rag Trade* was an early

1960s BBC TV sitcom set in a clothing factory where a militant shop steward, Paddy, repeatedly blew a whistle, shouting 'Everybody out!' at the slightest incident. So popular did the phrase in the strike-bound 1970s that the sitcom wound up being revived in 1977.) To me, this was beyond ridiculous. It was staggering to think that just one word, used in error by a secretary, could create a kerfuffle – or a walkout.

From then on, I treated the tape room 'boys' (none of them under 50, all dreaming of retirement from their very cushy job) with jokey but polite respect. This union stuff was way over my head. I'd had to be part of it to get myself here, but I really didn't want to get caught up in it in any way beyond that. It was just too… arcane.

It's bizarre, isn't it? Here was a very popular newspaper that, just like its rivals, ran sensational stories about sex, sport and murder, campaigned on its readers' behalf on all manner of issues and generally reflected the views and attitudes of the society of the times. Yet underneath what was essentially free speech in a centuries old democratic system was a tautly wound undercurrent of restriction. One wrong word from a clerical worker to a time-serving man waiting for his pension (and doing little else) and the entire enterprise wobbled. Madness (this national malaise was even echoed in a pop hit of 1973, The Strawbs' 'Part of the Union').

For most of that first year at the paper, I kept myself to myself socially, mostly because I had acquired a regular boyfriend, whom I saw two or three nights a week. James, in his mid-thirties, worked in a busy ad sales department in a magazine group. We'd met at my leaving drink in Covent Garden after my last day in the dull job. Nothing like my previous amours, he was upright, respectable, good looking in a formal sort of way with neatly trimmed dark hair and smartly dressed. He didn't have long hair over his collar like virtually all the other men, which troubled me a bit, but he was eager to take me out, mostly to restaurants, usually on his expense account, whenever I felt like it. If it sounds a bit one-sided, it was. He wasn't my type. Meaning there was no hint of danger, no sign of bad boy behaviour or subterfuge, no hedonistic dope-smoking or boozy habits – he restricted himself carefully to one beer in the pub, two glasses of wine at dinner – and therefore no challenge or excitement whatsoever involved in being around him.

At that point in 1972 – meeting James, starting the new job – I was still in a kind of limbo. Part of the plan in my reluctant move back to Dalston had been to save up enough money to get back on track and to share a flat again. This didn't quite happen as quickly as I'd planned because I'd run up a substantial bill on my first ever credit card, the Access, which had been launched to great fanfare that year alongside a mini-boom in banks releasing credit to the masses.

I'd gone mad with the new plastic, of course. I'd piled

into pricy gear from Young Jaeger and expensive Missoni tops from South Molton Street. Paying it all back was a struggle. It took ages. Yet I was determined to square things, no matter how much I hated being back home. Molly and Ginger, now resigned to my topsy-turvy behaviour, had remained sanguine. They seemed pleased when, months after I'd moved back, I told them about landing the job on the paper.

'Fleet Street? You mean Flea Street, doncha?' quipped Ginger.

This brief hiatus of stability – dating James, meeting him after work and heading for dinner in Soho to places like L'Epicure or the fashionable Carrier's restaurant in Islington's Camden Passage – was too safe, too predictable for me to ease into and be happy that I'd found a pleasant, easy, untroubled relationship for a change. In truth, there was nothing to criticise about James. An attractive bachelor boy, he was obviously intent on settling down, judging by the broad hints he'd drop from time to time, which I ignored.

For me, James was a sort of staging post, a place to stop briefly until I was ready to move on to another adventure. Yet the odd thing was, he didn't seem to pick up on my lack of enthusiasm for Project The Two of Us. It went right over his head. Over those lengthy dinners – he did enjoy his food – I'd told him much of my past history, none of which seemed to concern him. Or put him off. He'd just laugh and say something like. 'Well, you didn't know anyone like me, then, eh?' Meaning, 'I am your white knight, here to rescue you from all those pathetic bad boys.'

One topic that preoccupied him was buying a home. He was far from alone in this. By 1970 almost half of all British families were home-owners and a short-lived mini housing boom took place a couple of years later. James insisted on taking me to see his first purchase the minute he'd completed the transaction – a roomy, three-bedroom apartment in a red brick Edwardian block in north London.

He'd paid £15,000 for it, though in a few years' time the property market would crash and he'd be forced to sell it for the same price. It was a good apartment and, centrally located as it was, he hinted it would make a great first home for a working married couple. 'Yeah, if you're into that sort of thing,' I told him. I was more interested in finding a new flat to share now than following any dreams of domestic permanence via the housing ladder. Though I did condescend to stay there with him on the odd weekend. That suited me fine.

By summer 1973, a year after I'd joined the paper, I moved out of Dalston for good into a great new flat. Still in the St John's Wood area, this was a big, three-bedroom place above an estate agents' office in a small parade of shops in a pretty, tree-lined part of Boundary Road. Two sharers: a pretty, dark-haired Australian receptionist, Raelene, and a rather shy accountant, Richard. More maisonette living: an enormous kitchen and living room on the first floor and the bedrooms, two of them doubles, on the top floor opposite the loo and bathroom, plus a tiny box room.

Raelene had kept the lease on the place for some time and had originally shared the place with four other women. She told me she preferred to sleep in the box room to cut costs. The rent, £17 a week, meant Richard and I forked out £7 a week each for our big double rooms and Raelene the rest. A short walk from the bus stop and a five-minute ride to Baker Street tube, this was a steal. There was even an Indian restaurant below us for takeaways. Such eateries were now gradually making their mark on the nation's dining habits, alongside the boil in the bag Vesta curry, a culinary development I'd adopted with some enthusiasm. There was also a little French bistro in the parade of shops below us, La Goulue, for cheap candlelit dining if the situation demanded.

And it did. For Christmas 1973, I scooped up some bargain lurex leggings and a silky bronze crossover top from Martha Hill's little shop in Marylebone High Street and boogied the night away at the big office Christmas bash at the City Golf Club. From then on my partying habit resurfaced: pubs, drinking, followed by dinner in tiny restaurants. The exciting, thrill a minute, unpredictable times were back, fuelled by my new working environment where drinking was a way of life after work and where women who cared to participate in Fleet Street's drinking contest were made welcome.

There were quite a few one-night stands: I was even more indiscriminate than I'd been in the past, now that I had the freedom of my own big space again. It was a way of life I knew and, in all truth, enjoyed. The sheer unpredictability of social drinking and the way it loosens inhibitions still appealed to me. A lot.

Sometimes the one-nighters turned into friendships. Jose, a journalist in the London bureau of a big Spanish paper – rail thin, dark, suave but very, very serious, a political thinker – eventually became a good friend. All these encounters went into the social pot pourri with my old friends from around north London, the Fleet Street journapists (as Jenny dubbed them) and, of course, James, whom I still saw on and off.

For most of the time, it was pretty hectic. I'd often wind up stumbling into a taxi in the morning to get me to work quickly (price £3) because I'd been out partying until close to dawn. Sometimes I'd get home from the office, collapse into bed at 8 pm and sleep for 12 hours, just to catch up.

The Boundary Road flat was a shabbily furnished place but the big space and the two floors meant I never really saw much of my co-sharers. Which was just as well, because not long after moving in, I realised that Raelene was an unusually active woman. She was gorgeous looking: pint-sized, long, fair hair, slim figure and permanently tanned.

But her baffling lifestyle made my own partying instincts seem quite tame by comparison.

She wasn't the type to get pissed after work and see what happens, as I did. Oh, no. In fact, she didn't drink at all or do any drugs. Raelene was a collector. A collector of men, with whom she traded, non-stop, 24/7. Goods for services rendered is one polite way of putting it. But the actual nature of the transaction was unclear: I was never sure if she demanded hard cash – it seemed more like amateur hour: she wasn't a professional out-and-out hooker. She seemed to just collect men, taking whatever she could get from them at the time – a bottle of perfume, a scarf, a miniature liqueur bottle, anything. The receptionist bit was official cover for her other, collector-type activities. She hadn't worked full-time in any office since leaving her home town of Adelaide three years before. The girl was far too busy collecting men for a conventional nine-to-five job.

The first inkling of Raelene's trading practices came just after I'd moved in. Sound asleep, I was woken around 3 am by the insistent ringing of the phone, inconveniently installed at the foot of the stairs. Stumbling down, half asleep, I picked it up.

'Iz zat Raayleene?' came the voice loud and clear. 'Zis is Avi: I hav just arrived: you come see me now?'

'No it's not! She's not here, OK!' (Loud slamming of phone.)

Exactly the same thing happened again in the wee

hours a few nights later. Again, Raelene wasn't in her box room. Another foreign accent, another guy claiming he'd 'just got in London', obviously hoping to 'just get in Raelene'. Raelene was never around for me to ask her what this was all about. Then, about a week later, the same thing: a 2 am call. Yet this time, the voice had a distinctly Aussie drawl. Pissed off at being woken again but nonetheless curious, I grilled the guy. Yeah, he'd just got into London. Worked for Qantas. One of his mates had given him Raelene's number.

'Oh, so you know her from Adelaide?' I queried.

'Nah. Never met her. I'm at the Britannia. D'you fancy a beer, then?'

Now the penny was starting to drop. At work, I discussed it with Andrew, one of the younger reporters in the newsroom. Andrew wore white John Lennon-type suits and fancied himself as a bit of a raver, though personally I had my doubts about this. 'It's obvious, isn't it? She's handing out her number to all the airline crews,' he chortled. 'Gotta meet this girl. Can you bring her down the pub?'

Conversations with Raelene never seemed to get you very far, so I didn't bother to question her. I couldn't work out if she just acted dumb or really was genuinely quite dumb. Richard seemed very timid, quite in awe of us, scuttling away into his room the minute he got home, so I rarely engaged in much talk with him. Typically nosy, I peeked inside Raelene's little cubbyhole one day when she was out. What I found was startling confirmation that I really was sharing with a collector.

The tiny room was crammed, top to bottom, with a chaotic jumble of packages – clothing, perfume bottles, plastic bags, parcels in shiny gift wrap, bottles of expensive body lotion, gift boxes of soaps, all clearly accumulated over the years. Virtually every surface of the cramped 10ft by 8ft bedroom was covered with the evidence of Raelene's jackdaw instincts. It was obvious these were gifts from grateful admirers. A shrink would have had a field day with all this. Parcels, boxes, little packages are stuffed into every drawer or shelf in the landlord's cheap wardrobe, all shoved in, willy-nilly, among her clothes, with yet further booty shoved underneath the bed. Still more stuff is strewn around on the floor, completely covering the thin carpeting, making it quite difficult to walk across without squashing a box or tripping over something.

Only the little single bed remained visible to the eye as a sitting surface, yet this too had been commandeered as storage space, with several recently acquired gifts strewn over the threadbare, pink chenille bedspread. Everywhere I looked there was evidence of Raelene's desirability: bottles of duty free spirits and liqueurs, packets of M&S tights (are some men that mean?), After Eights, Cadbury's Milk Tray, bars of Toblerone, necklaces, costume jewellery clipped onto cardboard displays, long silk scarves of the hippie variety, hats, caps, slinky robes –

a virtual Aladdin's cave of Raelene's trophies. It wouldn't have surprised me if somewhere inside the clutter, you'd find books of Luncheon Vouchers. Didn't south London madam Cynthia Payne take LVs from her elderly clients in the late '70s? It was a pretty surreal sight. *A Life of Grime* hadn't made it to our TV screens at that time. If it had, the producers would have been hot footing it to film Raelene's Room, or Raelene's Pit as one wag dubbed it later on.

A week or so later after my reconnaissance of the Pit, I arrived home early one night to face yet more evidence of Raelene's world. A strange man was sitting at the kitchen table, a half-finished cup of tea in front of him. He was bearded, wearing a black jacket and a white shirt. But he was in his somewhat capacious underpants: his black trousers were neatly folded over a kitchen chair. There was a little black skull cap on the back of his head. He nodded at me, a tad nervously, when I walked into the kitchen, but didn't say a word. For a second, I was puzzled. Then I realised. He was a rabbi, a Jewish minister. I'm quite ignorant about many things about my own faith, but he was definitely a rabbi. I bounded up the stairs. Raelene was just exiting the bathroom, a towel wrapped around her head.

'What are you *doing*?' I yelled. 'What's this rabbi bloke doing in the kitchen?' (I wanted to say, 'And why are his trousers hanging over the chair?' but it was pretty obvious, really.)

'Oh, he's really nice,' she cooed innocently. 'I met him in Oxford Street. He's so sweet. He gave me a box of lovely chocolates, so I invited him back for a cup of tea.'

Logical really, isn't it? Meet a rabbi on Oxford Street, he hands over choccies. Then you invite him home to remove his trousers? For choccies? Just as well I hadn't got home earlier, to witness Raelene showing her gratitude by deploying what might have been a kitchen hand job, but was probably a blowjob. Over a cuppa. A Linda Lovelace moment. (Lovelace was the star of the famed oral sex movie, *Deep Throat*. Essentially a porn movie about a girl whose clitoris resides in her throat, the movie became a global phenomenon and arrived in the UK in 1973.)

This was all very odd, but I was in no position to judge her. Like me, Raelene was a woman of the times we were living in, the sex-charged 1970s. She couldn't get away with all this in her home town for sure, but given London's relative anonymity, she could just do what she liked without censure. A censor of any kind in Blighty was out of a job by then. This was true of newspapers as well. Working on a tabloid, I didn't pore over most of the copy I ran off for distribution in the newsroom (secretaries were not permitted to type up copy, as a result of the union's power). In truth, I rarely even bothered to actually read the paper when it came out, which wasn't unusual. 'I just look at it to check my byline, gal,' shrugged Jeff, a cheeky young reporter on the desk.

Yet it was impossible not to be aware of the overtly sexual influences that millions were now regularly digesting with their morning cuppa. There was Chesty Morgan, the American stripper with the amazing 73-inch bust (incredibly, all her own, nothing to do with surgical enhancement). Then there was the huge press brouhaha and scandal around the big Marlo Brando movie, *Last Tango in Paris*, with its notorious scene in which Brando makes love to Maria Schneider and raids the fridge for butter as a lubricant for anal sex, causing morality campaigner Mary Whitehouse to demand the film be banned. (It wasn't.) And people had flocked to see the infamous 'was it real or were they acting?' lovemaking scene with Julie Christie and Donald Sutherland in the movie *Don't Look Now*. The former British reticence around matters sexual had gone for a Burton. The zeitgeist now was increasingly along the lines of Badfinger's 1970 hit 'Come and Get It'.

It turned out Raelene also liked the shared experience. Not long after the rabbi incident, I pushed open the bathroom door after getting home and found Raelene and a skinny, long-haired American guy, splashing about in the bath, huge grins plastered all over their faces. 'Oops, sorry,' I said, already diving out of the door.

'Hey, baby!' he yelled behind me. 'Come and join us. Get in. We can make a sandwich, honey!'

Raelene giggled. Clearly, my flatmate really was up for

anything any guy ordained. Orgy? Any time. Quick blowjob? Just give me a minute to finish my makeup.

As time went on, there were more glimpses into Raelene's habits. On Sundays, she'd dive out of the flat on two or three separate 'dates' with different men, returning home after an hour or two. A guy would ring our doorbell mid-afternoon and stand there, out on the pavement in Boundary Road, bristling with erotic expectation. Raelene, forever running late, would trip down the stairs, all smiles, skimpily dressed for the outing whatever the weather, greeting the lucky chap with a big 'Hi' and a hug. Yet it would be glaringly obvious that despite the warmth of her greeting, she'd never ever set eyes on this guy before. I might go in for one-nighters on a whim, but that's really about it. No orgies for me, thanks.

CHAPTER ELEVEN

THE SPY WHO LOVED ME

O h, he's so smooth, this handsome older man: a shock of white hair, a dazzling smile, an old world, European, courtly manner. Wow. He's impressive. Quite glamorous, really. His name is Georgi and he's some sort of literary icon in his own country, a playwright, a man of letters. 'You must come to meet me for a drink at Bush House,' he tells me in his sexily accented English. Bush House was home of the BBC World Service. Yes, here's my number. You bet.

Meeting this man was no accident. It was a direct consequence of my Ibiza trips. In early 1974, in a tiny bar in trendy, hippie Santa Eulalia, with the haunting, atmospheric sound of *Tubular Bells* in the background and the evocative scent of wood smoke in the air, I met a Russian, a man originally from behind what was then known as the iron curtain. Anton was a defector from Communist Russia. A blond, dashing motorcycle champion, he'd been one of the privileged elite, a Russian who was actually permitted to travel outside the Soviet Union. Ordinary people were very much trapped by the tough Communist regime of those times – only trusted members of the elite, such as sportsmen and ballet dancers, were permitted to travel outside the USSR, as it was called then.

Effectively, a 20-something Anton followed the example of Rudolf Nureyev, the ballet superstar who had defected in spectacular fashion from his native Russia while on a trip with the Kirov Ballet in 1961. In Paris, Anton declared his desire to swap Mother Russia and Communism for the West. The suspicious French thought his story was dodgy, that he was a Soviet spy. They threw him in prison for 18 months. Once released, he hot footed it to Munich and a job as a journalist on Radio Free Europe, a US-funded radio station which broadcast pro-West material to the Soviet-dominated Eastern bloc countries.

Yet Anton had wound up, a few years later, as a part-time DJ in Ibiza. Why? He said he disliked the formal way of life in Germany. The climate in Munich didn't suit him. Fluent in several languages, he was irresistibly drawn to the sun and the hedonistic hippie life as a DJ in Ibiza. Well, that was his story… I was intrigued by Anton, his tale and his yearning for his homeland, to which he could never return. It helped too that he was good-looking, with long blond hair and an athlete's body. We had a short but sizzling affair, hence my three trips there in under a year, though by my last summer trip the sizzle had died down somewhat on both sides. At the time, I didn't question his story. It was only later that I began to see that things might not have been quite the way he told them.

Back home in London, and at Anton's insistence after we'd first met, I phoned one of his friends from Radio Free Europe, a very glamorous American woman called Anne, who lived nearby in a Baker Street flat. Anne, a divorcee, had a managerial job in the radio station's London office. Welcoming and friendly, delighted to have news of Anton (who I guessed might have been her lover too at some point), she immediately invited me round for drinks, introduced me to a couple of her other defector friends who also worked for Radio Free Europe.

I met Oleg, a movie director, who had defected in London's West End, walked into Savile Row police station and, unable to speak much English, let it be known by wild gestures that he sought refuge here. 'My best memory of that time was how nice the policemen were,' he told me. 'They sat me down and gave me a cup of tea. That was when I knew I'd be OK.'

Naturally, I was even more intrigued by all this. Yet the most fascinating of Anne's defector chums was the courtly, white-haired man in his forties. He was from Communist Bulgaria. After meeting him at Anne's place, I joined him at the BBC's Bush House for lunch. A few weeks later, he invited me to his book-lined garden flat in south London where we wound up in bed, not that surprising given his devastatingly seductive European charm.

A journalist working for the Bulgarian section of the World Service, Georgi had a story that was even more riveting than Anton's. A leading writer in Bulgaria with impeccable credentials, he had initially defected in Bologna, Italy, where his brother lived. Then in 1969 he'd decided to come to Britain. Highly critical of the Communist regime in his native country, especially those at the top, he'd repeatedly made openly critical broadcasts to Bulgaria about all this via the BBC World Service and Radio Free Europe. 'I tell the truth about what happens there, so people can know who their leaders really are. But the leaders in Bulgaria are very angry about me. They want to kill me,' he told me that day in south London.

I thought it was all very dashing and exciting, this defector stuff – quite brave really, running in desperation into the arms of another country because your own was so awful. I'd grown up with stories about the Cold War. Stalin was a 1950s household word for repression and the miserable lives of people living in the countries behind the iron curtain. In 1956, the

Hungarians had defied their Communist bosses and paid a terrible price, with thousands killed. And, of course, everyone knew about the British spies Burgess and McLean, privileged Brits who'd sold secrets – and their souls – to the Communists.

Yet the idea that someone actually wanted to kill one of these fascinating men, none of whom seemed remotely spy-like to me, seemed so far-fetched, so beyond what I understood about such things other than from James Bond movies. Kill this man, now working at good old Auntie BBC? He was just trying to impress me, I thought afterwards. Who'd want to kill a journalist here in grimy old south London? It was bullshit, I decided. We spoke on the phone once or twice after that time, yet I never saw Georgi again.

But Georgi wasn't spinning me a yarn. Nor was he trying to impress me. It was all too true. A few years later, in 1978, the name Georgi Markov made headlines all over the world. Standing at a London bus stop en route to his job at Bush House, Georgi felt a sharp pain, like a sting, at the back of his thigh. He looked round to see a man bending down to pick up a dropped umbrella. Then the man jumped into a taxi and sped away.

A few days later, Georgi died in a London hospital, leaving a widow and a small daughter. He had been poisoned. Traces of ricin, a deadly poison with no known antidote, had been lodged in a pin-sized metal pellet embedded in his calf. It is believed the tip of the umbrella being held by the man behind Georgi contained the deadly poison. It's widely believed that the authorities in Bulgaria had wanted this journalist dead, silenced for ever, and that they'd found an assassin to do their deadly work. It turned out to be one of the most infamous episodes of the Cold War, and Georgi's assassin has never been found.

For all my tough East End talk and bravado, I knew very little of international politics. I was drawn to these defector people, innocently enough, because I was so curious about everyone, especially those who came from other countries. Yet it never occurred to me that their lives, once they'd run away from Communism and their own country, might have involved a certain amount of compromise, a trade-off of information in return for safety in the West. Espionage, in a way. Iron curtain defectors, then, often brought added value, as they call it now, because they had usually been privileged insiders in the Communist world. They weren't really ordinary people. They'd had good connections in their homeland, so they were usually sought after by the US authorities. And it was the Americans who then funded Radio Free Europe, the station that had hired Ramon, Anne and Georgi.

Moreover, as a friend pointed out to me some time later, I worked for a British national newspaper. I wasn't a journalist, but I knew many journalists – and Anne, in particular, was exceptionally keen to meet my friends from the office, even inviting a few of them into her home. I took it all at face value, but later the big question was: had my innocent romance in Ibiza linked me to a chain of people who had traded East-West information? And was Anne's friendship, seemingly so willingly given, actually a way of getting closer to people who might have been useful, like my hack pals? There are still no clear answers. And I never questioned people's motives then.

On reflection, though, Anton surely wasn't quite what he said he was. Franco's strict Fascist regime in Spain at that time meant the local police in Ibiza would have known exactly who he was and where he came from. On one occasion, wandering around Ibiza town together, we were stopped by a man in a suit who demanded to see my passport. Naturally, I wasn't carrying it with me. Anton murmured to me that the man wanting my passport was a plainclothes policeman – and explained to the man, in Spanish, that the passport was at my hotel. The man said something curt and walked away.

'What did he say?' I asked Anton.

'He said this time it's OK, but if it happens again, there'll be trouble.'

This baffled me at the time. Ibiza is a small island and the man obviously knew Anton: he didn't ask for his papers. A while later, it occurred to me that Anton could easily have been working for the authorities there. He was perfectly placed for keeping an eye on the tourists and the many foreigners living and working there, many of whom were well to do and smoking lots of dope. Anton never touched or mentioned drugs. Yet I could never understand how he managed to run a car and a decent flat on a tiny, seasonal income as a DJ. He often said he was broke, but it still didn't quite add up.

By the end of that year of spies and Ibiza, my view of my life was changing. Even with breaks to the idyllic Mediterranean island, the novelty of my job, the working routine, was starting to lose its lustre, though there was no real reason for this other than my own habitual restlessness. On the news desk, Monty left to take his dream job as a racing correspondent. His replacement was Graham, a much quieter, more serious news editor, less prone to noisy, irreverent pronouncements. As his two hand maidens, the change in boss didn't really affect Jenny and me. We were treated with the same courtesy, did the same things. Yet for some of the reporters it was a bit unsettling. Journos tend to view all changes of senior management with great suspicion and Monty had been very popular: a hard act to follow. A few of the younger reporters on the desk were initially apprehensive about the change. The old hands took it all in their stride: they were safe in their jobs, thanks to the mighty union. But the younger ones were still finding their way, so they became unbelievably obsequious in their dealings with their new boss.

Once he'd settled in, Graham moved some reporters to

sit much closer to the news desk, which made the less favoured even more twitchy. Then he opted to have his own special little office constructed on the edge of the newsroom. This was followed by ordering a special humidifier to be placed by his desk. All this caused great consternation among the troops, though Graham did have a point: the lingering effect of cigarette smoke and a heating and ventilating system that didn't work properly made for an unhealthy fug.

Before long the office jokers had dubbed Graham's new office the Bollock Box, because it was assumed that was where he'd take reporters to give them a dressing down, and the humidifier became the Humiliator.

Technically, Jenny and I didn't work for the reporters, so this wave of change and the very noticeable, almost feet-kissing reverence for the new boss made for much ribbing of our colleagues. 'You're a bunch of toadies,' we chanted endlessly, exploiting any opportunity to send them up. The best moment came when Jenny devised her own implement of reporter torture – a wooden ruler with a big cut-out image of a speckled toad stuck on top.

Jenny would wait until the reporter was summoned by Graham for a newsroom chat, position herself so that only the reporter could see her and then bob up and down briefly, flashing the toady board each time as the pair chatted. It worked like a charm. The reporters struggled every time to keep a straight face while talking story tactics with the boss. So good was the toady board that one reporter had to ask to be excused, dashing off to the loo to unleash his mirth.

In another inspired move, Jenny soon amended the toady board and labelled it 'Toad of the Week', flashing it up and down for the reporters to see. More hilarity. We were always laughing – at someone else's expense, of course. It was quite childish. But then offices where people muck around a lot are often childish places, aren't they?

As for the reporters and photographers, their day to day exchanges – beyond office politics – mostly involved swapping yarns about jobs they'd been on, last night's leg-over or gleaning advice on the fastest way to achieve this. Here's a sample of a pub conversation between a youthful red-headed snapper, nicknamed the Orange, and Norman, one of the veteran Cockney reporters.

The Orange, chubby and very much single, fancies a holiday on the French Riviera. What does Norman, a well-travelled hack who knows all the fleshpots of Europe, think his chances of pulling are? 'If you go hunting for nookie on the Riviera, you're up against the best-looking French and Italian waiters,' warns Norm. 'You'll only get shitty tables and you'll end up having a wank. Go to Ireland instead. All you'll need to do is buy the bird a couple of gin and tonics and you can't miss. Go to Monaco and you'll end up wanking.'

Yet outside the confines of the cosy, close knit, joke-infested world of the newsroom and the pub, the bold black headlines of all the newspapers were repeatedly telling a somewhat depressing story: the notion that Britain was going to the dogs had started to become all-pervasive. Not just the strikes and the three-day week (of January to March 1974) to save electricity supplies, the soaring oil prices and the almost daily carnage of the sectarian war in Northern Ireland, now spilling over onto the mainland. That was all bad enough but prices had gone up 20 per cent in 12 months. Crime had risen alarmingly and the economy was in dire straits. I had mostly ignored all this, busy organising the next party, the next trip to the sunshine, my horizons virtually unaltered since the heady days of the late '60s.

In one way, I had prolonged my youth way beyond its sell-by date. So almost imperceptibly, at some point in 1975 the effect of what was going on in the wider world started to sink in and made me question my environment. At the same time, there was an increasing realisation that this Fleet Street life, certainly the best fun at work I had ever known, was a bit of a cosy trap. My restless nature, propelled by a determination to have no responsibility other than to enjoy myself and put myself about, had been given free reign. I'd morphed from '60s *Cosmo* girl into '70s pub girl, landing in a place where a secretary couldn't be thrown out for taking a three-hour lunch. With any number of funsters around me to share the party. Yet eventually I started to wonder about what lay ahead. Of course I did. I was nearly 30.

What I didn't understand about myself until much later was that I thrived on fresh challenges, not comfortable landings. I got bored far too quickly. I didn't do complacency. I also didn't realise that intellectually there was zero satisfaction in my work, so virtually all my nervous energy went into being a party animal – because I didn't know what else to do. It was the easiest option.

I wasn't struggling for some sort of career because the idea of a career, either in journalism or anything else, just didn't come into the equation. As for real independence, unwittingly I thirsted for it – but I didn't have it. I paid my own way for the basics – rent, clothes, bills and holidays – but everything else, all entertainment costs if you like, came from the opposite sex, who didn't question this. I would have loved to rent a nice flat on my own but I didn't earn anything like enough to cover the rent. I wasn't a Raelene. But neither was I financially independent. Ordinary secretaries didn't go out and buy flats, cars, or trips to the Caribbean then. The only available option for me if I wanted to sink into some sort of comfortable, alternative niche was... marriage.

I am wide awake at 3 am, Sunday morning. Next to me, James is snoring his head off. I've been staying with him this weekend, a fairly rare occurrence after several months of just seeing him for the odd dinner date, slotting him in occasionally, knowing full well that while I'm fond of the guy, respect his stability, his plodding determination to do a good job at work, make his way

240

up the ladder, I am just dangling him, keeping him interested while I enjoy myself elsewhere.

He knows and understands this. But he loves me. That's the nub of it. Typically English, he only blurts this out when he's had a few. I boozily mumble something in return, like 'Yeah, me too.' Hardly a declaration of passionate devotion. Yet he is blindly impervious to the fact that essentially this feeling is not mutual – he'd be better off looking for love elsewhere.

There are very rare moments in life when a brief flash of insight stops you in your tracks and you fully take in the truth of where you are heading. Or how you are really feeling and how you should proceed. About half a dozen of these moments have been significant personal signposts in my life. This is one of them. I lie there, staring at the moulded ceiling, thinking it all through, for once managing to ignore the irritating snores. Fact: marriage to James is on the cards. He hasn't done the bended knee, formal thing but he's made it glaringly obvious that's how he views us, that's what he wants. He doesn't want children. He knows I don't want children. He likes the good life, the comfortable home in the smart area, the lively, expense account working life in publishing, the regular travel and so on. I like these things too, of course. Who doesn't?

So why on earth shouldn't I do this? Why don't I join the respectable, the conventional throng, pair up, do the expected thing? By then, I have quite a few girlfriends who have waited until their late twenties or early thirties to tie the knot. Some have had to wait for a divorce to come through now that the laws have changed. Others have gone out and enjoyed themselves while a long-time love has remained in the background, dithering endlessly until the final decision.

The glib, snap answer to my dilemma is: well, you don't love him, so forget it. I don't have this romantic, girlie attachment to such easy answers. I'm enough of a cynic about love to know that it may or may not last, whatever the circumstances. I know for sure that my parents would be over the moon with sheer relief if I marry utterly respectable, responsible James. He's made it plain he is desperate to meet them, show them he's my protective knight in flared trousers, a kipper tie and even a Jason King moustache (which doesn't suit him, though he has grown his hair longer, at my insistence).

'Just do it,' a little voice tells me. 'It's time, isn't it?'

Then, with a flash of clarity, it strikes me. If I do this, do I make myself happy? No. I'm merely observing the convention, doing the convenient thing because I'm 30. And James? Will I make him happy? Of course not. I'm too restless, too all over the place emotionally, never mind my penchant for sleeping with whomever I fancy. That's two unhappy people. It would be utterly, totally selfish to take this man's offer to satisfy convention, give my parents what they crave: a sense that I'm stable, looked after.

'I wouldn't give it more than a year,' my other, rational voice whispers in my ear.

It's a truly big moment for me. Many people view my party girl instincts with wry amusement. 'But what do you *really* want, Jac?' I'm asked over and again. I can never answer them. I honestly don't know what it is I do want. It's out there, somewhere, this thing that I do want. But it is not, alas, contracting myself to a man who is a safe bet and loves me. I can't do this to him or myself.

My decision made, I decide to say no more, just keep him at arm's length until he gets the message. Wrong. All this does is prolong the agony. He's so patient. James phones, I say I'm busy. He keeps trying. And so on. Nearly six months passes. In the meantime I'm embroiled in yet another diversion with a twice-married northerner, Clive, a reporter on the *Sun*. He's a lively, sunny Leo who suits my fiery Sagittarius temperament perfectly. (I've been very keen on star signs and their significance ever since reading the massively popular American book called *Linda Goodman's Sun Signs* in the late '60s.)

Clive's a lively chatterbox – and chatter-upper. He's down to earth, open, affectionate and a very enthusiastic lover, unlike the other Fleet Street men I've sampled, most of whom are far too under the influence to even perform, let alone properly. I don't trouble myself overmuch that he's married with a wife in a distant suburb because a) it's much more exciting not knowing for sure when we'll meet up and b) in a way, it's a safer option right now than a single guy with marriage on the brain. And it suits me: I still want to hang onto my freedom of choice.

We fight a lot, Clive and I. Then we make up passionately. Anyone who has ever read Charles Bukowski, the American postman–turned-author (played by Mickey Rourke in a movie called *Bar Fly*) will know the scenario. Fight. Shout. Yell at each other. Make up. Screw. And so on...

One night, I'm waiting in the Printer's Devil wine bar for Clive to join me. Everyone knows about us, mostly because we fight so much in the pub. Even the barman starts singing 'Oh, I've got the *Sun* in the morning and the moon at night,' when I walk in. As I wait for Clive, my eye settles on a secretary I know. She works for one of the editorial bosses and has done for years. Their long-term affair (he won't leave his wife) is known to all. And there she sits on the bar stool, her gin and tonic half drunk, neatly dressed, patiently waiting for him to finish work at 10 pm. She's much older than me, mid-forties, a really nice woman. They're together during the week in a flat he rents nearby, then on weekends he's back in his lovely home, 30 miles outside London with his family.

We have the briefest of chats. She shrugs, a wry half-smile. 'They've got problems with the printers tonight. I s'pose he'll turn up in a bad mood,' she says gloomily, staring into her glass.

This is no way to live, I think to myself, even if you do love someone to bits. And there and then, just as I'd had that flash of insight in James' flat a few months before, I get another flash. It's obvious. This stuff can't go on, I tell myself. There's no way I want to be like her, sitting on a bar stool in Fleet Street at 40.

Fine. You don't want marriage and you don't want to remain in Fleet Street – even though it's a fairly cushy niche with a ready-made family of colleagues to laugh and gossip with. Can you come up with a good alternative? The answer, of course, is always the same. I want to travel and be free. Nice. 'But where will you go and how will you do it?' asks the little inner voice. Brick wall. I have no idea. Then Clive, curly-haired and thirsty after his shift, is at my side.

''Ello luv, sorry I'm late,' he says, rumpling my hair... and my big question remains dangling, unresolved and unanswered. For now. Off we go, out into the chilly night, hailing a taxi to Boundary Road, temporary partners in an inky dance of lust and living for the moment hedonism, our destinies propelling us forward towards two sides of the same coin: tragedy and success await us both, in a manner neither of us can predict. And it will all be happening quite soon, because neither of us is destined to remain working here, in this place, the land of the legless and the long lunch. That night, in a way, I spot my real future. I just don't know enough about the world, or myself, to be able to read the map.

CHAPTER TWELVE

MANY RIVERS TO CROSS

The food is going in the bin. Half-cooked sausages, blackened lamb chops, tomatoes, the lot, dumped straight into the garbage. The garden looks like a bomb has hit it. Chaos. Plastic chairs and beer cans litter the lawn. Mustard, tomato sauce and relish now mingle with the grass. Susan sighs heavily, stomps into the kitchen and starts to attack the washing up, venting her feelings on the greasy crockery. In the bedroom, the culprit, Ronald William, lies on the bed in T-shirt and shorts, out cold. A planned Sunday summer barbecue in Hampstead village has turned into a lost weekend. Ron, returning from the Wells after a heavy session, decides to get the barbie going. Susan, sensibly, suggests he wait until the guests arrive later on. A noisy argument follows. Ignoring Susan's entreaties, Ron lights the barbie, cursing its inefficiency, starts plonking the food onto it, pushing it around, even though the barbie's not quite hot enough.

Then the guests ring: 'Sorry, can't come.' By this time, Ron has chugged more Fosters. Then, rather predictably, he loses it, both with the somewhat useless Brit barbie and the ungrateful guests for whom he shopped heavily the day before. 'Fuckin' Poms! Typical!' he rants, picking up and throwing the half-cooked food around with considerable abandon. 'Give 'em a decent feed and they can't be assed to get out of fuckin' bed!' And so on.

Now he's sleeping it off, the sleep of the outraged and very plastered Aussie male. Susan fumes while I make coffee in the tiny kitchen, trying to bring her down. She sheds a few tears. Again, I do my best to console her. Just a few hours later, we're all three glued to the news on the telly: there's a big siege taking place right in the middle of London. The Spaghetti House Siege, as it became known, started that Sunday night when a trio of gunmen attempted an armed robbery in a Knightsbridge restaurant, holding nine Italian staff hostage in the restaurant basement for six days until the staff were finally released unharmed. When the news ends, Ron leaps up, switches off the TV. He is now completely sober, showered, dressed – and hungry.

'C'mon, you two sheilas! Let's go down the Shahbag for a tandoori!'

Susan and I look at each other: can you believe this guy? Then we all burst out laughing. It's a typical Ron scenario. Get pissed, create havoc, shout, rant – and pass out. Then it's all over. And quickly forgotten.

I've been close friends with these two for well over a year now. This kiss-and-make-up barbie-bashing is not unfamiliar. Ron is a wild child, a 6ft 3in reporter, mid-twenties, from a distant place called Broken Hill. He's been creating mayhem from Melbourne to Hong Kong and then London for a few years. The stories about him are legion. One night in the Melbourne newsroom at *The Herald* he decided to ring a former prime minister of Australia to blast him with a four-letter word invective. Later, while working on a Hong Kong radio station, Ron headed for Macau one night and a gambling session. Afterwards, well oiled and curious about what lay beyond the Macau border with China, he picked up a bike on the street and cycled across the border into China, a somewhat risky manoeuvre back then. Crashing his bike into a tree, he passed out. He awoke in a Chinese jail, surrounded by somewhat bemused Chinese guards, wondering what on earth they could do with this strange giant of a man. While the People's Republic deliberated, Ron played cards with the guards. The story made headlines across Australia. IT WAS THE BEST CHINESE MEAL I EVER HAD ran the strapline.

Since then, he's been employed as a casual in Fleet Street, mostly on investigations for the *News of the World*. He adores Susan, met in a Fleet Street bar not long after he arrived. They promptly set up home together in Willow Road near Hampstead Heath. She's a copy taker on the *Evening Standard*, the first woman to be permitted to do this job (someone took on the union and won). A lean, tall, glamorous, late 20-something from Kent, she's fallen heavily for her antipodean giant. When he's pissed, Ron is the archetypal Aussie oaf, smashing, crashing and cursing the Poms, their grey skies and warm, watery beer. The rest of the time, he's terrific company: witty, gregarious, kind-hearted and surprisingly domestic – he's a superb cook. In true Aussie style, Ron tends to tell it like it is. Susan is equally down to earth, though she's not anything like as personally insulting as Ron. I find the razor-sharp insults hilarious but many people can't handle it (think of the crushing honesty of a blast from Simon Cowell and you get the general idea).

'Agh, you expect every bloke to put the hard word on you,' he admonishes me when I complain that so-and-so seems immune to my charms. The 'hard word' is Aussie for attempting to proposition someone. (This is a pretty mild insult but it gives you the flavour.) He's *so* right. I can't quite get it into my head that I'm no longer 21 and sylph-like: I now teeter precariously between a size 12 and 14 (more 14), thanks to my eating and drinking habits. Yet only Ron throws the truth at me in this way, makes me see myself head on.

I enjoy hanging out with them: their smart little garden flat in the basement of a big house has become a weekend refuge for me when my own adventures start to pall. I confide in them too about my love life, though it's mostly Susan who listens and offers advice. Because we all work newspaper hours, we usually share our Mondays off, mostly spent lunching and boozing, ringing other lunchers to join the party or organising big meals in my flat (I even cook a bit now) and taking the piss mercilessly out of Raelene's antics.

Yet if Raelene is hopefully not a typical representative of her homeland, the lively young Australians I meet in Fleet Street strike me as being somewhat refreshing compared to the motley crew of hacks crowding the pubs in and around the Street. The Aussies are on a holiday of sorts, in London to work casual shifts for a while, getting a taste of the Fleet Street experience for their CVs before travelling on or moving back home. They don't take it all seriously – unlike all the staff journos or local freelancers who are completely wedded to their jobs and what the bosses are saying, to the point where the endless shop talk becomes irksome.

Aussies adore nicknames: the Chook, Argos, GB and Harpic (meaning round the bend) are Ron's gang. Ron's nickname is the Stone Fish, after a species found in Australian waters and one of the most dangerous fish in the world (its venom contained in its spine). It's easily trodden on because it looks like a rock. And it can kill. To be honest, I don't think Ron is truly dangerous: more an incautious boozer, a wild man. But also one who's a dab hand with a roast dinner and has an obsession with a clean kitchen plus an endearing habit of jumping up and reciting Aussie poems at the dinner table. I'd never heard of Banjo Patterson until then, Australia's famous bush poet. It's all hugely entertaining. Through my friendship with Ron and Susan, I relate to these Australians as instant party people, laconic humorists, turning up at the door en masse, grinning and clutching their cans of Party Four.

Underneath all this there is an ongoing confusion in my mind. I hunger for a next step, yet I can see no way of changing things. I definitely don't want to quit Fleet Street and find a new job in London. That, to me, seems pointless. In an attempt to clear the decks, as it were, I finally come clean with James that autumn. I haven't seen him for weeks or slept with him for months. In the Printer's Pie, we have what he clearly hopes is some sort of reunion. 'Look, I'm seeing someone else,' I blurt out, after he's ordered his usual steak and kidney pie. I needed three glasses of Hirondelle under my belt.

'I bet he's a journalist. And he's married,' James says quietly. How well he knows the environment I work in. Then, to my horror, I realise there are tears in his eyes. 'I loved you,' he says stupidly. Then, in a very James-type gesture, he takes out a clean white hanky, sniffs into it and then wipes the moisture off his face, regaining some composure.

Oh, no. What a horrible selfish cow. I shouldn't have

put this off. He obviously still had hopes. Yet I can't bring myself to placate him, be nice. I don't want to. What's the point? There's an awful silence. Then our food arrives. Still not speaking, we start eating. More silence, broken only by the noise of James chomping his food (an irritating habit that drives me mad) and the clatter of cutlery on plates. It's agonising. Then I put my knife and fork down. I have to say something, anything. 'We can still be friends, if you want,' I mumble.

'Thanks,' he says, clicking his fingers at the waiter for the bill (another infuriating habit), desperate to get away, even though his meal is half finished. Then he digs into his wallet, throws a £10 note onto the tablecloth and pushes back his chair. 'You sort it out. I'm going home.'

I justify it all to myself, of course. I've loved and lost in my time, haven't I? Now it's my turn to say, 'Sorry, no thanks.' Perhaps I did use him as a sort of available handbag, while I put myself about. Don't all women do that sometimes? I had treated him badly, I knew that. It would have been worse if we'd wound up married or living together, I tell myself.

We have one mutual friend, Big Pete, another ad sales guy. A few months after the Printer's Pie dinner, I run into BP in Fetter Lane. 'James has had quite a bit of bad luck,' he tells me. It seems James has been running around town with all sorts of different women. Then he's been stopped and breathalysed for drink-driving near Berkeley Square. Result: loss of licence, a bit of a blow for James. 'I shouldn't tell you this, Jacky, but he also told me he'd got a dose of the clap from one of these girls. He's a stupid bastard sometimes.'

Since many people were now bed-hopping like mad, the clap or a sexually transmitted disease like gonorrhea was frequently mentioned in conversation at that time in the '70s. Condoms became passé: many women were now on the pill or, like me, had an inter-uterine device fitted. 'A dose' was seen as a mere occupational hazard for shaggers. Bad luck, nothing more. Usually easily treated with antibiotics. Only when the AIDS virus surfaced in the early '80s did most people really start to take sexually transmitted diseases more seriously and understand the merit of the packet of three.

Through that summer of 1975 there have been other, more serious things going on in my life. After years of ignoring doctor's warnings about his blood pressure, my dad, Ginger, got sick. Smoking, drinking and being overweight have taken their toll. He had a stroke and wound up in the Metropolitan hospital in Kingsland Road, Dalston. He's lost some use of one arm and it affects his walking, though he can still get out and about enough to wander up the road and back. But he has had to stop working at the BMA. At 63, he's been pensioned off.

'Ging loved that job,' my mum tells me sadly one afternoon when I meet her in town after she's finished work at Berketex. With my dad now at home, she'll have to find part-time work in a local shop. She'll miss the bustle of Oxford Street and the lively shop talk, the company of all the other women working there.

'He's lucky to be here, Mum,' I tell her. And I don't say it, but I think he is very lucky to get the BMA pension so late in life. It means they aren't facing an impoverished old age.

Visiting them at the flat now is even sadder for me. Ginger has become like an old man, waiting for his demise. He isn't supposed to drink at all now and his sole pleasure is the almost daily trek to the betting shop in Shacklewell Lane, where he regularly runs into Michael, my friend Larraine's Italian husband. 'That Michael,' he'll say. 'What a lovely bloke he is.' This is rich. When we were in our teens, he'd hated my friendship with Lolly and her family. And when she'd married Michael, he'd been very derisive about Italians: 'Cowards, the lot of them.'

Now, with his enforced retirement and their shared love of the gee-gees, Michael's stock has soared in my dad's eyes. But I guess he just misses male company. At the BMA, he'd been a real favourite with the doctors, travelling up to Scotland with them for conferences, a kind of Cockney mascot for the august institution. Now all he has are four claustrophobic walls and my mum. And, of course, his old insecure possessiveness.

I am no longer a target because I am not there. But Molly will arrive home from her part-time job in the

High Road to find him either hanging out of the window or downstairs, in the street, worrying himself stupid if she's just a few minutes late from work. Stoically, as ever, she puts up with it, saying nothing.

I take all this on board. I'd been shocked to see him in a hospital bed, frail and helpless. In fact, the one time I'd visited him there, I'd burst into tears when the doctors drew the curtains around his cubicle. It surprised me: after all, I'd loathed his very existence for the better part of my life. But there is truth in the saying blood is thicker than water. At that point I'd realised that whatever I felt about his behaviour, our home, he was still my dad – the skinny man who'd dumped his bags in the hall, arriving back from India after WWII and, for a short while, someone I'd looked up to as a tiny tot. There was no getting away from that.

The changes come thick and fast that autumn. Not long after the Spaghetti House Siege and the day of the wrecked barbie, Susan rings me at the office. 'We're going to Australia, Jacky. I'll get a visa as Ron's partner and Ron says it'll be really easy for us to get work there. Ron's fallen out with the *News of the World*, anyway. He says he's had enough of Fleet Street.'

Boyfriends and lovers have come and gone over the last few years, but the imminent departure of two people I've come to regard as surrogate family is as much a shock to me as witnessing my dad's frailty. Within a few weeks they are gone, following a series of farewell lunches and dinners in Hampstead, our favourite Greek restaurant in Camden Town and a final, enormous goodbye lunch thrown by our friends running the Camden Head pub in Islington.

'Ya'd better think about coming out to Australia,' Ron tells me as we hug goodbye. 'You're going nowhere here.' Typical Ron, straight and to the point. I *was* going nowhere and the days were now shortening. Gloom was everywhere. The UK in the '70s had become synonymous with IRA car bombs. Suspect packages. Bomb scares where buildings were hastily evacuated. In central London, two people were killed by an IRA bomb at the Hilton Hotel that September. The following month a man was killed by an explosion at a bus stop in Green Park. A TV presenter and political activist, Ross McWhirter, was assassinated by the IRA outside his home in November. The bad news just went on and on. My mood, already quite flat, now plummets even further with the next piece of news: the end of an era on the newsdesk.

Jenny is expecting, a truly happy event for her and Roy. Their lives are changing. No longer will they be going off to concerts at weekends, buying expensive leather belts with 'The Eagles Tour' notched in silver at the back. It is time to be responsible parents. They've already bought a home and now Jen is giving up work. They're even going to tie the knot. 'I'm leaving in March,' she tells me delightedly. I join in the jokey congratulations and smiles. It should be good news. I'll move up a grade. As the senior, I'll do all the double time overtime on Friday nights, effectively a 20 per cent pay rise of about £10 a week. Instead, it plunges me into more confusion. I'll miss Jenny. We've laughed so much together – is there any better way to bond with colleagues? And we've always looked out for each other, though we're totally different people. I just can't envisage being there with a new person, a stranger.

Only Clive, always cheerful and optimistic, lifts my spirits. Sometimes he'll be sent away on a job for a few days and I manage to join him. That autumn, we go to Jersey, where he's been sent on a follow-up to a terrible story about the 'beast of Jersey', a man who had terrorised women and children on the Channel island for years, raping and assaulting them while wearing a ghastly rubber mask and studded wristbands. Edward Paisnel had been finally caught in 1971 and imprisoned for 30 years. Yet, in true Fleet Street style, the story didn't end there, mostly because he'd affected the lives of so many on the small island.

We have an uproarious few days in St Helier. Clive's trail of interviewees runs cold quite quickly so we make the most of the time, enjoying the hotel and room service. Although Clive is sympathetic to my dilemma, he doesn't have any solutions or ideas for me. 'If you leave the Street, luv, we'll never see each other,' he warns me.

But I am far from being the only restless soul. Around

me, quite a few 20- or early 30-somethings feel like me, that the UK is a basket case and if you can get out for a better life, now is the time to do it, if you aren't tied down by mortgages and family. We've all had a taste, by now, of what life can be like beyond the grey skies and scruffy pubs. The decade we'd lived through as 20-somethings had given us much freedom – and the cheaper travel explosion had turned many heads. Already, in the office, one or two older journos have retired to the sun in Spain. Some young freelancers are heading off to LA to try their hand at writing about the rich and famous for the tabloids. 'We can file our copy from the beach,' they tell everyone.

A few of the reporters on the desk are being lured to the USA by tabloids like the *National Enquirer*, who tempt them with an expenses-paid month's trial at the paper's Florida HQ. Journalists, by trade, were more itinerant then than now: there were more jobs, for a start, and foreign coverage on papers was more extensive in the pre-electronic era, so people could take chances as stringers if they fancied unfamiliar surroundings. But it wasn't just Fleet Street that was affected by this get up and get out feeling. All over the country, people wanted out.

It was one afternoon in early December when I finally found my get out of jail card. It was around 4 pm, the skies outside already darkening and the prospect of another winter of discontent looming large when a reverse-charge call came through to the news desk from the switchboard. We always accepted such calls, no matter where they came from, in case they meant good stories. 'I have a Mr Sinclair in Sydney for you. Will you accept the charge?' said the voice on the switch. Oh joy. Ron and Susan, in their new home by the beach. Well past 3 am there and they were full of the joys of it.

'Oh, Jac, you'd love it here' trilled Susan. 'They've got these amazing cardboard boxes with wine in them. You just put them in the fridge, push the button and it comes out lovely and cold. And wine's so cheap, it's incredible.' On and on they went, taking it in turns to tell me what a good time they were having. They'd found good jobs virtually on landing, Ron in radio for the ABC, the Aussie equivalent of the BBC, Susan doing typing shifts in the Radio Australia newsroom. They were renting a big roomy apartment for next to nothing. 'The money's so good, we've already started saving,' Susan told me. 'Last weekend we went to this amazing beach an hour's drive from the city: there was no one else there. We had the entire beach to ourselves.'

Oh, God. Empty beaches, cheap wine on tap, generous employers – how lucky could you be? Then it was Ron's turn to take the phone: he'd been drinking but he was still quite articulate. 'If you can get your ass here, you'll be laughing. They love Poms who've worked in Fleet Street. You'll walk straight into a job. And if you need money, we'll stump you for all the cash you need to get yourself a place until you get on your feet. I mean it. Think about it, eh?'

I've already mentioned my innate opportunism. It was there at the start of my working life and it never failed to propel me forward over time. I knew, for a start, that this was no idle comment. Ron, for all his wild, irreverent ways, had already sensed my ennui with my lot in life. Like many Australians, he genuinely believed in his lucky country and thought the Poms were a hapless lot, stuck in a grimy place where positivity, sunshine, good food and a decent living were in somewhat short supply. Put simply, he wanted to help. It was a generous gesture, made in spontaneity, certainly. But the offer was on the table.

I spent the entire weekend after the call in my flat, thinking about it all. Or rather, doing sums, plotting how I could scrape together enough money for the airfare. I could leave in March, with Jenny. I had to give three months' notice, anyway. We'd both say farewell together. That would give me plenty of time to save a bit. There was a pension fund I'd paid into. I could access that, which, combined with my outstanding holiday pay, would give me most of what I needed. It was definitely doable.

Once I'd found a job and a flat to share in Sydney, it'd take a bit of time to repay Ron. But I'd be in the sunshine, with two of my best friends. It was a fabulous offer. I immediately sent them a postcard to their new address: 'Want to come. Please ring the news desk again. I think I can get there after March. See you soon!' Yet I kept quiet about my plans. I wanted to be sure before I started making it all come true…

That Christmas Eve, I hailed a taxi from Fleet Street to Dalston. I'd overnight with Molly and Ginger in my old bedroom and break my news to them over Christmas lunch. I was quite worried about their reaction. Would Ginger start browbeating me, doing his possessive number: 'You can't do this to us,' 'We're your parents,' that sort of thing?

Amazingly, they took it well. 'I did my travel when I went to India,' said Ginger proudly. 'Now it's your turn. And you'll be back, anyway. You won't stick it there for long.' Gee thanks, Dad.

Molly was fine. She had long-lost relatives there. 'You can look them up, Jac.' I promised to do just that. One hurdle overcome.

I gave my notice in after New Year after several calls from Sydney during which we'd finalised all my plans. I'd go as a Brit tourist on a three-month visa and stay. 'No problem,' Ron assured me. 'They never check anything.'

He was half-right. My somewhat casual approach to paperwork, even in the pre- computer era, did go on to cause me problems down the line. But I wasn't about to let the details of immigration rules hold me up. I just wanted to get there.

'Well, Miss Hyams, you can show the Australians what

England is made of,' said Graham with a smile when I handed in my memo giving notice.

Brian, as ever, was completely sanguine. 'You'll be back, chummy,' he told me.

My other colleagues, mainly those who were quite happy to live out their lives to a Fleet Street sunset, were also less than encouraging. Australia was regarded very differently in 1976: a place seemingly full of 'colonials' with funny accents, lacking culture or couth. Yet few people had actually been there. Nearly everyone had a relative who'd gone off there to be a Ten Pound Pom (the nickname given to British migrants who'd opted to emigrate in the '60s, paying just £10 for their fare in return for two years in the former penal colony: if you left Australia before the two years were up, you paid your own fare back). A few had returned, deeply disillusioned.

'My aunt says it's a great place for doin' your washing,' said one pub wit.

'So and so says there are too many flies and not much else,' I was told.

One girl who'd worked there for a year and returned told me, 'Don't do it. It's a very strange place and people don't like you if you're English.'

'New Zealand?' said another pub pundit. 'It's a bit of a small place for someone like you, isn't it?'

Even Raelene wasn't exactly encouraging about her mother country. 'You'll like it for a bit, I s'pose, but you'll get bored if you stay much longer,' was her helpful comment.

Only Clive was enthusiastic about my forthcoming leap into the dark. Because he too was getting out, packing his bags. Amazingly, over Christmas he and his wife had made a similar decision to emigrate down under. Clive had recently fallen out of favour with his bosses for some unknown reason. They couldn't sack him but office politics meant that he'd get the crap jobs, rather than the travelling, the interesting stories. Because he worked for a paper owned by Rupert Murdoch, he'd already met one or two Australian executives, one of whom had already offered him a job on a Murdoch Sydney newspaper. It would all take time to organise, but he too would be in Australia by the middle of the coming year.

Strangely enough, this news left me with mixed feelings. I enjoyed being with Clive: it was impossible to be anything but cheerful and happy in his company. But it was always very much an affair, a Fleet Street one at that. I hadn't given too much thought to the Clive situation when I made my decision to decamp to the other side of the world. But still, I told myself, it would be reassuring to have yet another familiar face around.

I had absolutely no idea what to really expect when I landed in Australia. In the pre-electronic era, you only had photographs or movies to give you some idea of what it all looked like: mostly the images were of sprawling yellow beaches or dusty, alien outback places. There was the occasional news story from Oz, mostly involving sport. And, of course, the famed Ronnie Biggs, train robber extraordinaire, had run off there in 1966 to live with his family until his escape to Brazil in 1970.

'It's a fine place to make a film about the end of the world,' Ava Gardner had quipped to waiting reporters in Melbourne in 1959 when she arrived there to make a film called *On the Beach* – a movie about the last survivors of a nuclear holocaust. Judging by what I kept hearing in London, many still felt that way. Yet my enthusiasm remained undiminished. Ron's generous act of friendship gave me a chance to break free, do something different. In the sunshine, to boot. That was good enough for me. In many ways, it was a roll of the dice. Yet as usual, I ignored the what–ifs. Too much of that could hold you back.

I threw a series of farewell bashes: a remarkably sober one at the Cheshire Cheese off Fleet Street and a big boozy one at the flat for my north London friends, such as hippie Alan and his caravan of good-looking men and women from all points in the globe and Laurie, he of the ashtray smashing, now sleekly successful in PR with a mad, live-in girlfriend he desperately wanted to ditch. Anne turned up with Oleg in tow and even my quiet flatmate Richard produced his equally shy girlfriend and admitted he was moving out. They were getting married.

Everyone was either very stoned or smashed: the

reverbations of 'Goodbye Yellow Brick Road' and the joyful sound of the British Afro-pop band Osibisa echoed all the way down Boundary Road. Neighbours hammered on the door, demanding peace and quiet. It finally came at around 3 am. Raelene – egged on by Jeff and Roger, two reporters from the office who'd been pushing me for an introduction to her for ages – ran upstairs to the Pit. She emerged, minutes later, clad in her *piece de resistance*: an all-in-one pink and blue 'bunny' suit, with a cute little white bushy tail, covering a flap at the back – which revealed her naked bum.

'You guys wanna come upstairs?' she enticed in her broadest Oz tones. Two nigh-on legless young hacks didn't need any further encouragement: one waited outside the Pit while the other stepped inside briefly for Raelene's Linda Lovelace offering, her gifts for the younger generation of Fleet Street's finest.

'Did you have to take *two* of them on?' I asked Raelene the next night, after the lads had gleefully told the whole office about the event.

'Ah, what am I gonna do if he sticks it in ma mouth?' was her reply.

There was no answer to that.

A few days later, Jenny and I danced a farewell jig on the news desk, waving the reams of white copy paper and the news desk phones at the camera. I still have those photos. They show a very happy, high-cheeked 'Yoko' in a denim dress, long socks and two-toned pumps, delighted to be moving into the next important stage of her life. And alongside her, her co-worker, brown hair in a neat fringed bob, black roll-neck jumper, brown leather jacket and blue wide flares, looks straight at the camera and gives a half-smile, lips pursed.

The camera doesn't lie. You can see my apprehension, the uncertainty underneath it all. There would, indeed, be tricky, uncertain episodes after that day in March 1976 when the big bird went down the runway at Heathrow and took to the skies to transport me to the other side of the world. Yet my timing was impeccable. For me, it was exactly the right moment to put everything I knew behind me and make my way in the world in a totally different place. There will always be people in this world who need to leave their environment in order to reinvent themselves, flourish and become the person they never quite imagined they could be. My new horizons in Australia offered me so much more than a suntan, a new job and endless cask wine on tap.

As a relatively 'new' country, Australia had always been open, generous in opening its doors wide to people like me. The initial welcome was a bit shaky but after a while, I would be a true beneficiary of that open-handed, laidback Aussie generosity: a lucky Pom in a truly lucky country. In truth, it was all going to happen for me. A long, long way from home.